ROBERT GREENE
THE BLACKE BOOKES MESSENGER 1592

'CUTHBERT CONNY-CATCHER'
THE DEFENCE OF CONNY-CATCHING
1592

ELIZABETHAN AND JACOBEAN QUARTOS

ELIZABETHAN AND JACOBEAN QUARTOS
EDITED BY G. B. HARRISON

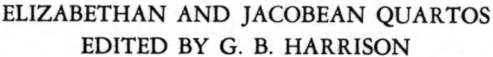

ROBERT GREENE, M.A.
THE BLACKE BOOKES
MESSENGER
1592

'CUTHBERT CONNY-CATCHER'
THE DEFENCE
OF CONNY-CATCHING
1592

BARNES & NOBLE, Inc.
New York, New York

This edition published in 1966
by Barnes & Noble, Inc.
is reproduced from the series
BODLEY HEAD QUARTOS
published by
John Lane The Bodley Head Ltd., London
between 1922 and 1926

Note

THE ORIGINAL of this text is in the Bodleian Library (Malone 575). A list of the misprints corrected in the text will be found on page 33.

G. B. H.

Printed in the United States of America

INTRODUCTION

THE *BLACKE BOOKES MESSENGER* is the fifth and last pamphlet which was written by Robert Greene to expose the professional rascals of London.

Greene began the attack in the autumn of 1591 with the *Notable Discovery of Coosnage*, in which he denounces 'Conny-catchers' (card-sharpers), crosbiters, and dishonest colliers. There can be no doubt that the pamphlet caused considerable sensation and did actually draw attention to the abuses attacked—to the disadvantage of the Conny-catchers. The *Notable Discovery* was soon followed by the *Second Part of Conny-catching*, with its second edition, *The Second and Last Part*,[1] which dealt with Nips, Foists, and other light-fingered gentry.

The Conny-catchers were now making preparations for a counter-attack. 'Marry,' writes Greene in the *Second Part*, 'the goodman Cony-catchers, those base excrements of dishonesty, report they haue got one, (   ) I will not bewray his name, but a scholler they say he is, to make an inuectiue against me, in that he is a fauourer of those base reprobats' (page 28).

But threats and opposition (which also meant advertisement) only encouraged Greene to produce the *Third and Last Part of Conny-catching*, which was founded—so he claims—on the experiences and observations of a magistrate. The book was entered in the Stationers' Register on 7 February, 1592.

On the 21 April *The Defence of Conny-catching* was entered. In the Address, 'Cuthbert Conny-catcher' advises Greene to deal with great abuses and to leave such humble offenders alone. He also adds a plain hint that any further disclosures would be made at his own peril. Greene's life was indeed in danger, and at least one determined attempt was made to murder him;[3] but he was no coward, and, in the fourth pamphlet, *A Dispvtation betweene a Hee Conny-catcher and a Shee Conny-catcher*, he did not hesitate to mention names and places. Finally he promised to publish a *Blacke Booke* which should include not only a directory of the addresses of receivers of stolen goods, but also a roll of all the 'Foystes, Nips, Lifts and Priggars in and about London.' And, as his enemies knew, Greene was in earnest.

[3] See the *Dispvtation*, pages 40–1.

INTRODUCTION

The announcement of the *Blacke Booke* naturally aroused much excitement both in the general public and in the Conny-catchers. On 21 August an entry in the Stationers' Register runs:

> John Danter   Entred for his copie vnder th[e h]andes of master Watkins and Master Stirrop / a booke intituled / *The Repentance of a Cony catcher* / with the *Life & death of [blank] MOURTON and Ned BROWNE, twoo notable cony catchers* / *The one latelie executed at Tyborne the other at Aix in Ffraunce.* . . . . vj^d
>
> *Arber's Reprint ii.* 619.

However disinterested his original motives had been, Greene had now realized that Conny-catching pamphlets were 'best-sellers.' Accordingly, after the manuscript had been entered, he decided to issue the *Life and Death of Ned Browne* as a separate volume, under the alluring title of *The Blacke Bookes Messenger*. But the supply of authentic stories was running short, and most of Ned Browne's exploits are manifestly fictitious, though the facts of his death are probably true. Indeed, Greene did not even hesitate to borrow ideas from his enemies' *Defence*.[4]

[4] Compare page 21 of *The Blacke Bookes Messenger* with page 34 of the *Defence*.

INTRODUCTION

But the sickness which he mentions in the *Address* to the *Blacke Bookes Messenger* was more serious than he had suspected. He grew rapidly worse, and died on 3rd September.[5]

Greene's death caused a great sensation, and several of the manuscripts found amongst his papers were published immediately, including *Greene's Vision* and the more famous *Groatsworth of Wit*, which was prepared for the Press by Henry Chettle. There can be little doubt that the real *Blacke Booke* was actually written, as Chettle, who was likely to know the truth about Greene's affairs, in his *Kind-hartes Dreame* makes 'Greene's Ghost' remark: 'For my Bookes, of what kind soeuer, I refer their commendation or dispraise to those that haue read them. Onely for my last labours [*i.e.* the Conny-catching pamphlets] affirming, my intent was to reproue vice, and lay open such villanies, as had beene very necessary to be made knowne, whereof my *Blacke Booke*, if euer it see light, can sufficiently witnesse.'

But the Conny-catchers had the last word, and the manuscript of the *Blacke Booke* disappeared.

G. B. HARRISON.

[5] For an account of the life and pathetic death of Robert Greene, see my *Shakespeare's Fellows*, chapter 2.

THE
BLACKE BOOKES
MESSENGER.

Laying open the Life and Death of *Ned Browne* one of the most notable Cutpurses, Crosbiters, and Conny-catchers, that euer liued in England.

Heerein hee telleth verie pleasantly in his owne person such strange prancks and monstrous villanies by him and his Consorte performed, as the like was yet neuer heard of in any of the former bookes of Conny-catching.

Read and be warnd, Laugh as you like, Iudge as you finb.

Nascimur pro Patria.
by R. G.

Printed at London by Iohn Danter, for *Thomas Nelson* dwelling in Siluer streete, neere to the signe of the Red-Crosse. 1592.

G. STEEVENS

To the Curteous
Reader Health.

GEntlemen, I knowe you haue long expected the comming foorth of my *Blacke Booke*, which I long haue promised, and which I had many daies since finished, had not sickenes hindered my intent: Neuerthelesse, be assured it is the first thing I meane to publish after I am recouered. This Messenger to my *Blacke Booke* I commit to your curteous censures, being written before I fell sick, which I thoght good in the meane time to send you as a Fayring, discoursing *Ned Brownes* villanies, which are too many to bee described in my *Blacke Booke*.

I had thought to haue ioyned with this Treatise, a pithy discourse of the Repentance of a Connycatcher lately executed out of Newgate, yet forasmuch as the Methode of the one is so far differing from the other, I altered my opinion, and the rather for that the one died resolute and desperate, the other penitent and passionate. For the Connycatchers repentance / which shall shortly be [A3

THE EPISTLE TO THE READER

published, it containes a passion of great importance. First how he was giuen ouer from all grace and Godlines, and seemed to haue no sparke of the feare of God in him: yet neuerthelesse, through the woonderfull working of Gods spirite, euen in the dungeon at Newgate the night before he died, he so repented him from the bottome of his hart, that it may well beseeme Parents to haue it for their Children, Masters for their seruants, and to bee perused of euery honest person with great regard.

And for Ned Browne of whome my Messenger makes report, hee was a man infamous for his bad course of life and well knowne about London: Hee was in outward shew a Gentlemanlike companion attyred very braue, and to shadowe his villany the more would nominate himselfe to be a Marshall man, who when he had nipt a Bung or cut a good purse, he would steale ouer in to the Lowe Countries, there to tast three or foure Stoapes of Rhenish wine, and then come ouer forsooth a braue Souldier: But at last hee leapt at a daysie for his loose kind of life, and therefore imagine you now see him in his owne person, standing in a great bay windowe with a halter about his necke ready to be hanged, desperately pronounsing this his whole course of life and confesseth as followeth.

Yours in all curtesie, R. G./ [A3ᵛ]

A Table of the words of Art late-
ly deuised by *Ned Browne* and his associates, to
*Crosbite the old Phrases vsed in the manner
of Conny-catching.*

HE that drawes the fish to the bait,	*the Beater.*
The Tauerne where they goe,	*the Bush.*
The foole that is caught,	*the Bird.*
Connycatching to be called,	*Batfowling.*
The wine to be called,	*the Shrap.*
The Cards to be called,	*the Limetwigs.*
The fetching in a Conny,	*bëating the bush*
The good Asse if he be woone,	*stooping to the Lure.*
If he keepe a loofe,	*a Haggard.*
The verser in conny-catching is called,	*The Retriuer.*
And the Barnacle,	*the pot hunter.*

THE LIFE AND
death of Ned Browne, a notable Cutpurse and Conny-catcher.

IF you thinke (Gentlemen) to heare a repentant man speake, or to tel a large tale of his penitent sorrowes, ye are deceiued: for as I haue euer liued lewdly, so I meane to end my life as resolutely, and not by a cowardly confession to attempt the hope of a pardon. Yet, in that I was famous in my life for my villainies, I will at my death professe my selfe as notable, by discoursing to you all merrely, the manner and methode of my knaueries, which if you hear without laughing, then after my death call me base knaue, and neuer haue me in remembrance.

Know therfore (Gentlemen) that my parents were honest, of good reporte, and no little esteeme amongst their neighbours, and sought (if good nurture and education would haue serued) to haue made me an honest man: but as one selfe same ground brings foorth flowers and thistles; so of a sound stocke prooued an vntoward Syen; and of a vertuous father, a most vicious sonne. It bootes

little to rehearse the pettie sinnes of my Non-age;
as disobedience to my parents, con / tempt of [B1
good counsaile, despising of mine elders, filching,
pettilashery, and such trifling toyes: but with these
follyes I inurde my selfe, till waxing in yeares, I
grew into greater villanies. For when I came to
eighteene yeares olde, what sinne was it that I
would not commit with greedinesse, what attempt
so bad, that I would not endeuour to execute;
Cutting of purses, stealing of horses, lifting, pick-
ing of lockes, and all other notable coossenages.
Why, I helde them excellent qualities, and ac-
counted him vnworthy to liue, that could not, or
durst not liue by such damnable practises. Yet as
sinne too openly manifested to the eye of the
Magistrate, is eyther sore reuenged or soone cut
off: So I to preuent that, had a nette wherein to
daunce, and diuers shadowes to colour my
knaueries withall, as I would title my selfe with the
name of a Fencer, & make Gentlemen beleeue that
I pickt a liuing out by that mysterie, whereas God
wot, I had no other fence but with my short knife,
and a paire of purse stringes, and with them in
troth many a bowt haue I had in my time In
troth? O what a simple oth was this to cõfirm a
mans credit withall? Why, I see the halter will
make a man holy, for whilest God suffered mee to
flourish, I scornd to disgrace my mouth with so

MESSENGER 7

smal an oath as In faith: but I rent God in peeces, swearing and forswearing by euery part of his body, that such as heard mee, rather trembled at mine oathes, than feared my braues, and yet for courage and resolution I refer my selfe to all them that haue euer heard of my name.

Thus animated to do wickednes, I fell to take delight in the companie of harlots, amongst whome, as I spent what I gotte, so I suffered not them I was ac/quainted withall to fether their nestes, [B1 *v* but would at my pleasure strippe them of all that they had. What bad woman was there about London, whose champion I would not be for a few Crownes, to fight, sweare and stare in her behalfe, to the abuse of any that should doo Iustice vpon her? I still had one or two in store to crosbite withall, which I vsed as snares to trap simple men in: for if I tooke but one suspitiously in her companie, straight I verst vpon him, and crossebit him for all the money in his purse. By the way (sith sorrow cannot helpe to saue me), let mee tell you a mery ieast how once I crosse-bit a Maltman, that would needes bee so wanton, as when hee had shut his Malt to haue a wench, and thus the Ieast fell out. [B2

B

A pleasant Tale how Ned Browne crossebit a Maltman.

THis Senex Fornicator, this olde Letcher, vsing continually into White Chappell had a haunt into Petticote Lane to a Trugging house there, and fell into great familiaritie with a good wench that was a freend of mine, who one day reuealed vnto me how she was well thought on by a Maltman, a wealthie olde Churle, and that ordinarily twise a weeke he did visite her, and therefore bad mee plot some meanes to fetch him ouer for some crownes. I was not to seeke for a quicke inuention, and resolued at his comming to crossebite him, which was (as luck serued) the next day. Monsieur the Maltman comming according to his custome, was no sooner secretly shut in the chamber with the wench, but I came stepping in with a terrible looke, swearing as if I meant to haue challengd the earth to haue opened and swallowed me quicke, and presently fell vpon her and beat her: then I turned to the Maltman, and lent him a blow or two, for he would take no more: he was a stout stiffe olde tough Churle, and then I rayld vpon them both, and obiected to him how long he had kept my Wife, how my neighbors could tell me of it, how the Lane thought ill of me for suffering it, and now that I had my self taken them together, I would make both him and her smart for it before we parted.

The olde Foxe that knew the Oxe by the horne, was subtill enough to spie a pad in the straw, and to see that we went about to crossebite him, wherefore hee stoode / stiffe, and denied all, and [B2ᵛ although the whore cunningly on her knees weeping did confesse it, yet the Maultman faced her downe, and said she was an honest woman for all him, and that this was but a coossenage compacted betweene her and me to verse and crossbite him for some peece of money for amends, but sith hee knew himselfe cleare, he would neuer graunt to pay one penny. I was straight in mine oathes and braued him with sending for the Constable, but in vaine, all our pollicies could not draw one crosse from this crafty olde Carle, till I gathering my wits together, came ouer his fallowes thus. I kept him still in the chamber, & sent (as though I had sent for the Constable) for a freend of mine, an aunceint coossener, and one that had a long time beene a Knight of the Post, marry hee had a faire cloake and a Damaske coate, that serued him to bayle men withall. To this periured companion I sent to come as a Constable, to make the Maltman stoupe, who (readie to execute any villanie that I should plot) came speedily like an aunceint welthy Citizen, and taking the office of a Constable in hand, began very stearnly to examine the matter, and to deale indifferently, rather fauoring the Maltman than me: but I complained how long he had kept my Wife, he answered I lyed, & that it was a coossenage to crossebite him of his money. Mas Constable cunningly made this reply to vs both: My frends, this matter is bad, and truly I cannot in conscience but look into it. For you *Browne*, you complaine how he hath abused your wife a long time, & shee partly confesseth as much: he (who seems to bee an honest man, and of some countenance amongst his neighbors) forswears it, and saith, it is but a deuise to strip him of his mony: I know / not whom to beleeue, and [B3 therfore this is my best course because the one of you shall not laugh the other to scorn Ile send you all three to the Counter, so to answere it before some Iustice that may take examination of the matter. The Maltman loth to goe to prison, and yet vnwilling to part from any pence, saide he was willing to answere the matter before any man of worshippe, but hee desired the Constable to fauour him that hee might not goe to ward, and he would send for a Brewer a friend of his to be his Baile.

In faith saies this cunning old Cosener, you offer like an honest man, but I cannot stay so long till he bee sent for, but if you meane as you protest to answer the matter, then leaue some pawne and I will let you goe whither you will while to morrow, and then come to my house here hard by at a Grocers shop, and you and I will goe before a Iustice and then cleare your selfe as you may. The maltman taking this crafty knaue to be some substantiall Citizen, thanked him for his friendship and gaue him a seale ring that he wore on his forefinger, promising the next morning to meete him at his house. Assoone as my friend had the ring, away walkes he, and while we stood brabling together he went to the Brewars house with whome this Maltman traded and deliuered the Brewar the Ring as a token from the Maltman, saying he was in trouble, and that he desired him by that token to send him ten pound. The Brewar seeing an auntient Citizen bringing the message and knowing the Maltmans Ring, stood vpon no tearmes sith he knew his Chapman would and was able to answere it againe if it were a brace of hundreth pounds, deliuered him the money without any more a/doo. which ten pound at night [B3^v we shard betwixt vs, and left the maltman to talke with the Brewar about the repaiment. Tush this was one of my ordinary shifts, for I was holden in my time the most famous Crosbyter in all London: Well at length as wedding and hanging comes by destenie, I would to auoide the speech of the world bee married forsooth and keepe a house, but

(Gentlemen) I hope you that heare mee talke of marriage, do presently imagine that sure she was some vertuous matrone that I chose out. Shal I say my conscience, she was a little snowt faire, but the commonest harlot and hackster that euer made fray vnder the shadowe of Colman hedge: wedded to this trull, what villanie could I deuise but shee would put in practise, and yet though shee could foyst a pocket well, and get me some pence, and lifte nowe and then for a neede, and with the lightnes of hir heeles bring mee in some crownes: yet I waxt wearie, and stucke to the olde prouerbe, that chaunge of pasture makes fat Calues: I thought that in liuing with mee two yeares she liued a yeere too long, and therfore casting mine eye on a pretty wench, a mans wife well knowne about London, I fell in loue with her, and that so deepely that I broke the matter to her husband, that I loued his wife, and must needs haue hir, and confirmd it with many othes, that if he did not consent to it, I would bee his death: whereuppon her husband, a kind Knaue, and one euerie way as base a companion as my selfe, agreed to me, and we bet a bargaine, that I should haue his Wife, and he should haue mine, conditionally, that I should giue him fiue poundes to boote, which I promised, though he neuer had it: so wee like two good Horse-corsers, made a choppe and / [B4 change, and swapt vp a Rogish bargaine, and so he maried my wife and I his. Thus Gentlemen did I neither feare God nor his lawes, nor regarded honestie, manhood, or conscience, but these be trifles and veniall sinnes. Now sir, let me boast of my selfe a little, in that I came to the credite of a high Lawyer, and with my sword freebooted abroad in the country like a Caualier on horsebacke, wherein I did excell for subtelty: For I had first for my selfe an artificiall haire, and a beard so naturally made, that I could talke, dine, and sup in it, and yet it should neuer bee spied. I will tell you there rests no greater villany than in this practise, for I haue robbed a man in the morning, and come to the same Inne and bayted, yea and dyned with him the same day, and for my horse that he might not be knowne I coulde ride him one part of the day like a goodly Gelding with a large tayle hanging to his feetlockes, and the other part of the day I could make him a Cut, for I had an artificiall taile so cunningly counterfeited, that the Ostler when hee drest him coulde not perceiue it. By these pollicies I little cared for Hues and Cries but straight with disguising myselfe, would outslip them all, and as for my Cloake it was *Tarmosind* (as they doe tearme it) made with two outsides that I could turne it how I list, for howsoeuer I wore it the right side still seemed to be outward: I remember howe prettily once I serued a Priest, and because one death dischargeth all, and is as good as a generall pardon, heare how I serued him./[B4ᵛ]

A merrie tale how Ned Browne vsed a Priest.

I Chaunced as I road into Barkeshire to light in the company of a fat Priest that had hanging at his saddle bow a capcase well stuft with Crownes that he went to pay for the purchase of some lands: Falling in talke with him (as communication will growe betwixt trauellers) I behaued my selfe so demurely, that he tooke me for a very honest man, & was glad of my company, although ere we parted it cost him very deare: and amongst other chat he questioned me if I would sell my horse (for hee was a faire large Gelding well spread and forheaded, and so easily and swiftly paced, that I could well ride him seauen mile an houre) I made him answere that I was loth to part from my Gelding, and so shapte him a slight reply, but before wee came at our baite hee was so in loue with him that I might say him no nay, so that when wee came at our Inne and were at dinner together we swapt a bargain: I had the Priests and twenty Nobles to boote for mine. Well assoone as we had changde I got mee into the stable, and there secretly I knit a haire about the horse feetlock so straight vpon the veine that hee began a little to checke of that foote, so that when he was brought foorth the horse began to halt; which the Priest espying marueld at it, and began to accuse me that I had deceiued him. Well quoth I tis nothing but a blood, and assoone as hee is warme hee will goe well, and if in riding you like him not, for twenty shillings losse, Ile change with you at night, the Priest was glad of this, and caused his sad/dle [Cr to be set on my gelding, and so hauing his Capcase on the saddle pummell, rode on his way, and I with him, but still his horse halted, and by that time we were two myles out of the towne hee halted right downe: at which the Priest chaft, and I saide I wondred at it, and thought he was prickt, bad him alight and I would see what he ayled, and wisht him to get vp of my horse that I had of him for a mile or two, and I would ride of his, to trie if I could driue him from his hault. The Priest thankt me, and was sorrowfull, and I feeling about his foote crackt the haire asunder, and when I had done got vp on him, smiling to my selfe to see the Capcase hang so mannerly before mee, and putting spurs to the horse, made him giue way a little, but beeing somewhat stiffe, he halted for halfe a mile, and then began to fall into his olde pace, which the Priest spying, said: Me thinks my

Gelding begins to leaue his halting. I marry doth hee Maister Parson (quoth I) I warrant you hele gallop too fast for you to ouertake, and so good Priest farewell, and take no thought for the carriage of your Capcase. With that I put spurres to him lustily, and away flung I like the wind: the Parson calde to mee, and sayde hee hoped that I was but in ieast, but he found it in earnest, for he neuer had his horse nor his capcase after.

Gentlemen, this is but a ieast to a number of villanies that I haue acted, so gracelesse hath my life beene. The most expert and skilful Alcumist, neuer tooke more pains in experience of his mettals, the Phisition in his simples, the Mecanicall man in the mysterie of his occupation, than I haue done in plotting precepts, rules, axiomes, and principles, how smoothly and neately to foist a pocket, or nyppe a bung./ [C₁ ᵛ

It were too tedious to holde you with tales of the wonders I haue acted, seeing almost they bee numberlesse, or to make report how desperately I did execute them, eyther without feare of God, dread of the Law, or loue to my Country: for I was so resolutely, or rather reprobately giuen, that I held Death only as Natures due, and howsoeuer ignominiously it might happen vnto mee, that I little regarded: which carelesse disdain to die, made me thrust my selfe into euery braule, quarrell,

and other bad action whatsoeuer, running head-
long into all mischiefe, neyther respecting the
ende, nor foreseeing the danger, and that secure
life hath brought me to this dishonorable death.
But what should I stand heere preaching? I liued
wantonly, and therefore let me end merrily, and
tel you two or three of my mad pranks and so bid
you farewell. Amongst the rest I remember once
walking vp and downe Smithfield, very quaintly
attired in a fustian dublet and buffe hose, both
layde downe with golde lace, a silke stocke and a
new Cloke, I traced vp and downe verie solempnly,
as hauing neuer a crosse to blesse me
withall, where beeing in my dumps
there happened to me
this accident
following./ [C2

A pleasant tale how Ned Brown kist a Gentlewoman and cut her purse.

THus Gentlemen beeing in my dumps, I sawe a braue Countrey Gentlewoman comming along from saint Bartlemewes in a satten Gowne, and foure men attending vpon her: by her side shee had hanging a maruellous rich purse embroydred, and not so faire without but it seemed to be as wel lined within: At this my teeth watered, and as the pray makes the thiefe, so necessity and the sight of such a faire purse beganne to muster a thousand inuentions in my heade how to come by it: to goe by her and Nip it I could not, because shee had so many men attending on hir: to watch hir into a presse that was in vaine, for going towards S. Iohns streete, I gest her about to take horse to ride home, because all her men were booted. Thus perplexed for this purse, and yet not so much for the boung as the shels: I at last resolutely vowed in my selfe to haue it though I stretcht a halter for it: and so casting in my head how to bring my fine Mistris to the blow, at last I performed it thus. Shee standing and talking a while with a Gentleman I stept before hir and leaned at the Barre till I saw hir leaue him, and then stalking towards hir very stoutly as if I had beene some young Caualier or Captaine, I met her

and curteously saluted her, & not onely greeted
her, but as if I had been acquainted with her I gaue
her a kisse, and so in taking acquaintance closing
very familiarly to her I cut her purse: the Gentlewoman seeing me so braue vsed mee kindly, &
blushing said, shee knew me not. Are you not
Mistres quoth / I, such a Gentlewoman, and [C2v
such a mans Wife? No truly sir, quoth she, you
mistake me: then I cry you mercie quoth I, and
am sorry that I was so saucily bolde. There is no
harme done sir sayde shee, because there is no
offence taken, and so we parted, I with a good
bung, and my Gentlewoman with a kisse, which
I dare safely sweare, she bought as deare as euer
shee did thing in her life, for what I found in the
purse that I keep to my selfe. Thus did I plot
deuises in my head how to profit my selfe, though
it were to the vtter vndoing of anie one: I was the
first that inuented the letting fall of the key, which
had like to cost me deare, but it is all one, as good
then as now: and thus it was.

How Ned Browne let fall a key.

WAlking vp and downe Paules, I saw
where a Noble mans brother in England
came with certaine Gentlemen his freendes in at
the West doore, and how hee put vp his purse, as
hauing bought some thing in the Churchyard: I

hauing an Eagles eye, spied a good bung containing many shels as I gest, carelesly put vp into his sleeue, which draue me straight into a mutinie with my selfe how to come by it. I lookt about me if I could see any of my fellow frends walking there, & straight I found out three or foure trusty foists with whom I talkt and conferd about this purse: wee all concluded it were necessary to haue it, so wee could plot a meanes how to catch it. At last I set downe the course thus: as soone as the throng grew great, and that there was Iustling in *Paules* for roome, I stept before the Gentleman and let fall a key, which stooping / to take vp, I staid [C3 the Gentleman that he was faine to thrust by mee, while in the presse two of my freends foisted his purse, and away they went withall, and in it there was some twentie pound in gold: presently putting his hande in his pocket for his handkercher, hee mist his purse, and suspected that he that let fall the key had it; but suppositions are vaine, and so was his thinking seeing he knew me not, for till this day he neuer set eye of his purse.

There are a number of my companions yet liuing in England, who beeing men for all companies, will by once conuersing with a man, so draw him to them, that he shall thinke nothing in the world too deare for them, and neuer bee able to parte from them, vntill hee hath spent all he hath.

If he bee lasciuiously addicted, they haue *Aretines* Tables at their fingers endes, to feed him on with new kind of filthines, they wil come in with *Rous* the french Painter, and what an vsuall vaine in bawdery hee had: not a whore or queane about the towne but they know, and can tell you her marks, and where and with whom she hosts.

If they see you couetously bent, they wil tel you wonders of the Philosophers stone, and make you beleeue they can make golde of Goose-greace: onely you must bee at some two or three hundred pounds cost, or such a trifling matter, to helpe to set vp their Styles, and then you need not care where you begge your bread, for they will make you doo little better if you followe their prescriptions.

Discourse with them of Countries, they will set you on fire with trauailing, yea what place is it they will / not sweare they haue beene in, and [C3ᵛ] I warrant you tell such a sound tale, as if it were all Gospell they spake: not a corner in *Fraunce* but they can describe. *Venice*, why it is nothing, for they haue intelligence from it euery houre, & at euery worde will come in with *Strado Curtizano*, and tell you such miracles of Madam *Padilia* and *Romana Imperia*, that you will bee mad tyll you bee out of England. And if hee see you are caught with that bait, he will make as though hee would leaue you, and faine businesse about the Court, or that such a Noble man sent for him, when you wil rather consent to robbe all your freends, than be seuered from him one hower. If you request his company to trauel, he wil say Infaith I cannot tell: I would sooner spend my life in your company than in any mans in England, but at this time I am not so prouided of money as I would, therefore I can make you no promise: and if a man should aduenture vpon such a iourney without money, it were miserable and base, and no man will care for vs. Tut, money say you (like a liberall young maister) take no care for that, for I haue so much land and I wil sell it, my credite is so much, and I will vse it: I haue the keeping of a Coosens chamber of mine, which is an old Counsellor, & he this vacation time is gone downe into the Country, we wil breake vp his studie, rifle his chests, diue into the bottome of his bags, but wee will haue to serue our turne: rather than faile, we wil sel his books, pawne his bedding and hangings, & make riddãce of all his houshold stuffe to set vs packing. To this he listens a little, & sayes: These are some hopes yet, but if he should go with you, and you haue money & he none, you will domineere ouer him at your pleasure, and then / he were well set vp, to [C4 leaue such possibilities in England, and be made a slaue in another Countrey: With that you offer to part halfes with him, or put all you haue into his custodie, before hee shoulde thinke you meant otherwise then well with him. Hee takes you at your offer, and promiseth to husband it so for you, that you shall spend with the best and yet not wast so much as you doe: which makes you (meaning simply) put him in trust and giue him the purse: Then all a boone voyage into the low Countries you trudge, so to trauel vp into *Italie*, but *per varios casus & tot discrimina rerum*, in a Towne of Garrison he leaues you, runnes away with your money, and makes you glad to betake your self to prouant, and to be a Gentleman of a Company. If hee feare you will make after him, hee will change his name, and if there be any better Gentleman than other in the Countrey where hee soiournes, his name hee will borrowe, and creepe into his kindred, or it shall cost him a fall, and make him pay sweetely for it in the end, if he take not the better heede. Thus will he bee sure to haue one Asse or other a foote, on whom hee may pray, and euer to haue newe inuentions to keepe himselfe in pleasing.

There is no Art but he will haue a superficiall sight into, and put downe euery man with talke, and when he hath vttered the most he can, makes men beleue that hee knowes tenne times more than hee will put into their heads, which are secrets not to be made common to euerie one.

He will perswade you hee hath twentie receiptes of Loue powders: that hee can frame a Ring with such a quaint deuise, that if a Wench put it on her finger, / shee shall not choose but followe you [C4v vp and downe the streetes.

If you haue an enemie that you would faine be ryd of, heele teach you to poyson him with your very lookes. To stande on the top of Paules with a burning glasse in your hande, and cast the Sunne with such a force on a mans face that walkes vnder, that it shall strike him starke dead more violently than lightning.

To fill a Letter full of Needles, which shall bee laide after such a Mathematicall order, that when hee opens it to whome it is sent, they shall all spring vp and flye into his body as forceably, as if they had beene blowne vp with gunpowder, or sent from a Calleeuers mouth like small shotte.

To conclude, he will haue such probable reasons to procure beleefe to his lyes, such a smooth tongue to deliuer them, and set them foorth with such a grace, that a very wise man he should be that did not swallowe the Gudgin at his hands.

In this sorte haue I knowne sundry yoong Gentlemen of England trayned foorth to their own destruction, which makes mee the more willing to forewarne other of such base companions.

Wherefore, for the rooting out of these slye

insinuating Mothworms, that eate men out of their substance vnseene, and are the decay of the forwardest Gentlemen and best wittes: it were to bee wished that *Amasis* Law were reuiued, who ordayned that euery man at the yeares ende shoulde giue account to the Magistrate how he liued, and he that did not so, or could not make an account of an honest life, to be put to death as a Fellon without fauour or pardon. /

Ye haue about London, that (to the disgrace of Gentlemen) liue gentlemen-like of themselues, hauing neythere money nor Lande, nor any lawfull meanes to maintain them: some by play, and they go amumming into the Countrey all Christmas time with false dice, or if ther be any place where gentlemen or Marchants frequent in the Citty or Towne corporat, thyther will they, either disguised like yonge Marchants, or substantiall Cittizens, and drawe them all dry that euer deale with them.

There are some doe nothing but walke vp & downe Paules, or come to mens shops to buy wares, with budgets of writings vnder their armes, & these will talke with any man about their sutes in Lawe, and discourse vnto them how these and these mens bonds they haue for money, that are the chiefest dealers in London, Norwich, Bristowe, and such like places, & complaine that they cannot get one penny. Why if such a man doth owe it you, (will some man say that knowes him) I durst buy the debt of you, let me gette it of him as I can: O saieth my budget man, I haue his hand and seale to shewe, looke here els, and with that pluckes out a counterfaite band, (as all his other writings are) and reades it to him: whereupon, for halfe in halfe they presently compound, and after he hath that tenne pound payd him for his band of twentie, besides the forfeiture, or so forth, he saies faith these Lawyers drinke me as drie as a siue, and I haue money to pay at such a day, and I doubt I shall not be able to compasse it. Here are all the Leases and Euidences of my Lande lying in such a shyre, could you lend me fortie pound on them till the next Tearme, or for some sixe / [D1ᵛ Monthes, and it shall then be repayd with interest, or Ile forfeit my whole inheritance, which is better worth than ahundred markes a yeare.

The welthy Gentleman, or yong Nouice, that hath store of Crownes lying by him, greedy of such a bargaine, thinking (perhaps) by one clause or other to defeate him of all he hath, lends him money, and takes a faire Statute marchant of his Lands before a Iudge: but when all comes to al, he hath no more land in England then a younger brothers inheritance, nor doth any such great Occupier as he faineth, know him: much lesse owe him any money: whereby my couetous maister is cheated fortie or fiftie pound thick at one clap.

Not vnlike to these, are they, that comming to Ordinaries about the Exchange, where marchants do table for the most part, will say they haue two or three shippes of Coles new come from Newcastle, and wish they could light on a good chapman, that would deale for them altogether. Whats your price saith one? Whats your price? saith another. He holds them at the first at a very high rate, and sets a good face on it, as though he had such traffique indeed, but after ward comes downe so lowe, that euery man striues who shall giue him earnest first, and ere he be aware, he hath fortie shillings clapt in his hand, to assure the bargaine to some one of them: he puts it vp quietly, and bids them enquire for him at such a signe and place, where he neuer came, signifying also his name: when in troth hee is but a coozening companion, and no such man to bee found. Thus goes he cleere away with fortie shillings in his pursse for nothing, and they vnlike to see him any more./[D2

A merry Ieast how Ned Brownes wife was crossebitten in her owne Arte.

BVt heere note (Gentlemen) though I haue done many sleights, and crossbitten sundry persons: yet so long goes the pitcher to the water,

that at length it comes broken home. Which prouerbe I haue seene verified: for I remember once
that I supposing to crosbite a Gentleman who had
some ten pound in his sleeue left my wife to performe the accident, who in the ende was crossebitten her selfe: and thus it fel out. She compacted
with a Hooker, whom some call a Curber, &
hauing before bargained with the Gentleman to
tell her tales in her eare all night, hee came according to promise, who hauing supt and going to bed,
was aduised by my wife to lay his clothes in the
window, where the Hookers Crome might crossbite them from him: yet secretly intending before
in the night time to steale his money forth of his
sleeue. They beeing in bed together slept soundly:
yet such was his chaunce, that he sodenly wakened
long before her, & being sore troubled with a
laske, rose vp and made a double vse of his
Chamber pot: that done, he intended to throw it
forth at the window, which the better to performe,
he first remoued his clothes from thence; at which
instant the spring of the window rose vp of the
owne accord. This sodainly amazed him so, that
he leapt backe, leauing the chamber pot still
standing in the window, fearing that the deuill had
been at hand. By & by he espyed a faire iron
Crome come marching in at the window, which in
steade of the dublet and hose he sought for, sodenly

tooke hold of that homely seruice in the member vessell, and so pluckt goodman Iurdaine with all his contents downe pat on / the Curbers pate. [D2ᵛ Neuer was gentle Angler so drest, for his face, his head, and his necke, were all besmeared with the soft sirreuerence, so as hee stunke worse than a Iakes Farmer. The Gentleman hearing one cry out, and seeing his messe of altogether so strangely taken away, began to take hart to him, and looking out perceiued the Curber lye almost brained, almost drowned, & well neare poysoned therewith: whereat laughing hartily to himselfe, hee put on his owne clothes, and gotte him secretly away, laying my wiues clothes in the same place, which the gentle Angler soone after tooke; but neuer could she get them againe till this day.

This (Gentlemen) was my course of life, and thus I got much by villany, and spent it amongst whores as carelessely: I sildome or neuer listened to the admonition of my freendes, neither did the fall of other men learne me to beware, and therefore am I brought now to this end: yet little did I think to haue laid my bones in *Fraunce*, I thought (indeed) that Tyburne would at last haue shakt me by the necke: but hauing done villany in England, this was alwaies my course, to slip ouer into the Low Countries, and there for a while play the souldiour, and partly that was the cause of my comming hither: for growing odious in and about London, for my filching, lifting, nipping, foysting and crosbiting, that euery one held me in contempt, and almost disdained my companie, I resolued to come ouer into *Fraunce*, by bearing Armes to winne some credite, determining with my selfe to become a true man. But as men, though they chaunge Countries, alter not their minds: so giuen ouer by God into a reprobate sence, I had no feeling of goodnes, but with the dogge fell to my / olde vomit, and heere most [D3 wickedly I haue committed sacrilege, robd a Church, and done other mischeeuous pranks, for which iustly I am condemned and must suffer death: whereby I learne, that reuenge deferd is not quittanst: that though God suffer the wicked for a time, yet hee paies home at length; for while I lasciuiously lead a carelesse life, if my friendes warned mee of it, I scoft at them, & if they told me of the gallowes, I would sweare it was my destenie, and now I haue proued my selfe no lyar: yet must I die more basely, and bee hangd out at a window.

Oh Countrymen and Gentlemen, I haue helde you long, as good at the first as at the last, take then this for a fare well: Trust not in your owne wits, for they will become too wilfull oft, and so deceiue you. Boast not in strength, nor stand not on your manhood, so to maintain quarrels; for the end of brawling is confusion: but vse your courage in defence of your country, and then feare not to die; for the bullet is an honorable death. Beware of whores, for they be the Syrens that draw men on to destruction, their sweet words are inchantments, their eyes allure, and their beauties bewitch: Oh take heede of their perswasions, for they be Crocodiles, that when they weepe, destroy. Truth is honorable, and better is it to be a poore honest man, than a rich & wealthy theefe: for the fairest end is the gallowes, and what a shame is it to a mans freends, when hee dies so basely. Scorne not labour (Gentlemen) nor hold not any course of life bad or seruile, that is profitable and honest, least in giuing yourselues ouer to idlenesse, and hauing no yeerly maintenance, you fall into many preiudiciall mischiefs. Contemne not the vertuous counsaile of a frend, / despise not the hearing [D3v] of Gods Ministers, scoffe not at the Magistrates, but feare God, honor your Prince, and loue your country, then God will blesse you, as I hope he will do me for all my manifolde offences, and so Lord into thy hands I commit my spirit, and with that he himselfe sprung out at the window and died.

Here by the way you shall vnderstand, that going ouer into *Fraunce,* he neare vnto *Arx* robd

a Church, & was therefore condemned, and hauing no gallowes by, they hangd him out at a window, fastning the roape about the Bar: and thus this *Ned Browne* died miserably, that all his life time had beene full of mischiefe & villany, sleightly at his death regarding the state of his soule. But note a wonderfull iudgement of God shewed vppon him after his death: his body beeing taken down, & buried without the towne, it is verified, that in the night time there came a company of Wolues, and tore him out of his graue, and eate him vp, where as there lay many souldiers buried, & many dead carcasses, that they might haue prayde on to haue filled their hungry paunches. But the iudgments of God as they are iust, so they are inscrutable: yet thus much we may coniecture, that as he was one that delighted in rapine and stealth in his life, so at his death the rauenous Wolues deuoured him, & pluckt him out of his graue, as a man not worthy to be admitted to the honor of any buryall. Thus haue I set downe the life and death of *Ned Browne*,
a famous Cutpurse and Conny-catcher,
by whose example if any be profited,
I haue the desired ende
of my labour. [D4]

FINIS.

ERRATA

The following emendations only have been made:—

Page	Line		In the Original reads:
2	2	'.'	','
6	25	'troth'	'torth'
7	21	'me)'	'me'
11	18	'would'	'wogld'
13	5	'sinnes'	'sinues'
19	22	'*key*.'	'*key*,'
22	24	'if he'	'ifhe'
25	11	'Gentlemen)'	'Gentlemen'
31	18	'mischiefs.'	'mischiefs'
31	18	'vertuous'	've rtuous'
31	28	'vnto'	'vnte'

The Defence
of Conny-Catching

Note

THE ORIGINAL of this text is in the British Museum (C. 40. b. 6). In this copy, instead of the *Address* here printed, the *Address* from Greene's own *Notable Discovery* has been substituted. The original *Address* has been restored from the copy of *The Defence* in the Henry E. Huntington Library, San Gabriel, California.

I wish to express my thanks to the Librarian of the Huntington Library for his kindness in supplying a photographic facsimile.

The list of misprints corrected in the text will be found on page 66.

G. B. H.

THE DEFENCE OF
Conny catching.
OR
A CONFVTATION OF THOSE
two iniurious Pamphlets published by *R.G.* against
the practitioners of many Nimble-witted
and mysticall Sciences.

By Cuthbert Cunny-catcher, Licenciate in Whittington Colledge.

Qui bene latuit bene vixit, dominatur enim
fraus in omnibus.

Printed at London by *A. I.* for *Thomas Gubbins*
and are to be sold by *Iohn Busbie*, 1592.

To all my good frends
health.

AS *Plato* (my good friendes) trauelled from Athens to Aegypt, and from thence through sundry clymes to increase his knowledge: so I as desirous as hee to search the deapth of those liberall Artes wherein I was a professour, lefte my studie in *Whittington Colledge*, & traced the country to grow famous in my facultie, so that I was so expert in the *Art of Cony-catching* by my continuall practise, that that learned Philosopher *Iacke Cuttes*, whose deepe insight into this science had drawn him thrise through euery gaole in England, meeting of mee at *Maidstone*, gaue mee the bucklers, as the subtlelest that euer he sawe in that quaint and mysticall forme of Foolosophie: for if euer I brought my Conny but to crush a potte of ale with mee, I was as sure of all the crownes in his purse, as if hee had conueyed them into my proper possession by a deede of gifte with his owne hande.

<small>Newgate builded by one Wittington.</small>

At *Dequoy, Mumchaunce, Catch-dolt, Oure le bourse, Non est possible, Dutch Noddie,* or *Irish one and thirtie,* none durst euer make compare with me

<small>The names of suche games as Connicatchers vse.</small>

for excellence: but as so many heades so many wits, so some that would / not stoope a farthing at [A2 cardes, would venter all the *byte in their boung* at dice. Therefore had I cheates for the very sise, of the squariers, langrets, gourds, stoppe-dice, highmen, low-men, and dice barde for all aduantages: that if I fetcht in anie nouyce eyther at tables, or anie other game of hazard, I would bee sure to strippe him of all that his purse had in Esse, or his credyt in Posse, ere the simple Connie and I parted.

> Al the monie in their purse.

When neyther of these would serue, I had consorts that could verse, nippe, and foyst, so that I had a superficiall sight into euery profitable facultie. Insomuch that my principles grew authenticall, and I so famous, that had I not beene crost by those two peeuish Pamphlets, I might at the nexte Midsommer haue worne Doctor *Stories* cappe for a fauor. For I trauelled almost throughout all England, admired for my ingenious capacitie: till comming about Exceter, I began to exercise my art, and drawing in a Tanner for a tame Conie, assoone as he had lost two shillings he made this replie. Sirha, although you haue a liuery on your backe, and a cognisance to countenance you withall, and beare the port of a Gentleman, yet I see you are a false knaue and a Connycatcher, and this your companion your setter, and that before you and I part Ile proue.

> Some Conicatchers dare weare noblemens liueryes, as W. Bickerton and others.

TO THE READERS

At these wordes Conny-catcher and Setter, I was driuen into as great a maze, as if one had dropt out of the clowds, to heare a pesant cant the wordes of art belõging to our trade: yet I set a good face on the matter and asked him what he ment by Cony-catching. Marry (q. he) althogh it is your practise, yet I haue for 3. pence bought a litle Pamphlet, that hath taught me to smoke such a couple of knaues as you be. When I heard him talke of smoaking, my heart waxed cold, and I began to gather into him gently. No no sir (q. he) you cãnot verse vpon me, this booke hath taught me to beware of cros-/biting: And so to be [A2ᵛ breefe he vsed me curteously, and that night causd the Constable to lodge mee in prison, & the nexte morning I was carried before the Iustice, where likewise he had this cursed book of Conycatching, so that hee could tel the secretes of mine art better then my selfe: whereupon after strict examination I was sent to the gaole, & at the Sessions by good hap & some friend that my money procured mee, I was deliuered. Assoone as I was at liberty, I got one of these bookes, & began to tosse it ouer very deuoutly, wherin I found one art so perfectly anotomized, as if he had bene practitioner in our facultie forty winters before: then with a deepe sigh I began to curse this *R. G.* that had made a publike spoyle of so noble a science, and to exclaime against that palpable asse whosoeuer, that would make any pen-man priuy to our secret sciences. But see the sequel, I smoothered my sorrowe in silence, and away I trudged out of Deuonshire, & went towards Cornwal, & comming to a simple Ale-house to lodge, I found at a square table hard by the fire halfe a doozen countrie Farmars at cardes. The sight of these pennyfathers at play, draue me straight into a pleasant passion, to blesse fortune that had offred such sweet opportunity to exercise my wits, & fil my purse with crowns: for I coũted all the mony they had, mine by proper interest. As thus I stood looking on them playing at cros-ruffe, one was taken reuoking, whereat the other said; what neighbour wil you play the cony-catcher with vs? no no, wee haue read the booke as wel as you. Neuer went a cup of small beare so sorowfully down an Ale-knights belly in a frosty morning, as that word stroke to my hart, so that for feare of trouble I was fain to try my good hap at square play, at which fortune fauoring mee, I wan twenty shillings, and yet doe as simply as I could, I was not onelie suspected, but called Conny-catcher and crosse-biter. / [A3

But away I went with the money, and came presently to London, where I no sooner arriued amongst the crue, but I heard of a second parte

TO THE READERS

worse then the first, which draue mee into such a great choller, that I began to enquire what this *R. G.* should bee. At last I learned that hee was a scholler, and a Maister of Artes, and a Conny-catcher in his kinde, though not at cards, and one that fauoured good fellowes, so they were not palpable offendors in such desperate lawes: wherevpon reading his bookes, and surueying euery line with deepe iudgement, I began to note folly in the man, that would straine a Gnat, and lette passe an Elephant: that would touch small scapes, and lette grosse faultes passe without any reprehension. Insomuch that I resolued to make an Apologie, and to aunswere his libellous inuectiues, and to proue that we Conny-catchers are like little flies in the grasse, which liue: or little leaues and doe no more harme: whereas there bee in Englande other professions that bee great Conny-catchers and caterpillers, that make barraine the field wherein they baite.

Therfore all my good friends vouch of my paines, and pray for my proceedings, for I meane to haue about with this *R. G.* and to giue him such a veny, that he shalbe afrayd heereafter to disparage that mysticall science of Conny-catching: if not, and that I proue too weake for him in sophistrie, I meane to borrowe *Will Bickertons* blade, of as good a temper as *Morglay* King *Arthures* sword was, and so challenge him to the single combat: But desirous to ende the quarrell with the penne if it be possible, heare what I haue learned in *Whittington* Colledge,

> *Yours in cardes and dice*
> Cuthbert cony-catcher./ [A3ᵛ

THE DEFENCE OF
Conny-catching.

I Cannot but wonder maister *R. G.* what Poeticall fury made you so fantasticke, to wryte against Conny-catchers? Was your braine so barraine that you had no other subiect? or your wittes so dried with dreaming of loue Pamphlettes, that you had no other humour left, but satirically with *Diogenes*, to snarle at all mens manners? You neuer founde in *Tully* nor *Aristotle*, what a setter or a verser was.

It had been the part of a Scholler, to haue written seriously of some graue subiect, either Philosophically to haue shewen how you were proficient in *Cambridge*, or diuinely to haue manifested your religion to the world. Such triuiall trinkets and threedbare trash, had better seemed *T. D.* whose braines beaten to the yarking vp of Ballades, might more lawfully haue glaunst at the quaint conceites of conny-catching and crossebiting.

But to this my obiection, mee thinkes I heare your maship learnedly reply, *Nascimur pro patria*: Euery man is not borne for himselfe, but for his

country: and that the ende of all studious indeuours ought to tende to the aduancing of vertue, of suppressing of vice in the common-wealth. So that you haue herein done the part of a good subiect, and a good scholler, to anotomize such secret villanies as are practised by cosoning companions, to the ouerthrow of the simple people: for by the discouery of such pernitious lawes, you seeke to roote out of the common-wealth, such ill and licentious liuing persons, as do *Ex alieno succo viuere*, liue of the sweat of other mens browes, and vnder subtil shiftes of witte abused, seeke to ruine the flourishing estate of Englande. These you call vipers, moathes of the common-wealth, caterpillers worse then God rayned downe on Egypt, rotten flesh which / must be diuided from the whole. [A4
Ense resecandum est ne pars sincera trahatur.

This maister *R. G.* I know will be your answere, as it is the pretended cause of your iniurious Pamphlets. And indeede it is very well done, but greater had your praise been, if you had entered into the nature of more grosse abuses, and set downe the particular enormities that growe from suche palpable villanies. For truth it is, that this is the Iron age, wherein iniquitie hath the vpper hande, and all conditions and estates of men seeke to liue by their wittes, and he is counted wisest, that hath the deepest insight into the getting of gaines: euery thing now that is found profitable, is counted honest and lawfull: and men are valued by theyr wealth, not by their vertues. Hee that cannot dissemble cannot liue, and men put their sonnes now a dayes Apprentises, not to learne trades and occupations, but craftes and mysteries.

If then witte in this age be counted a great patrimony, and subtletie an inseparable accident to all estates, why should you bee so spitefull maister *R. G.* to poore Conny-catchers aboue all the rest, sith they are the simplest soules of all in shifting to liue in this ouer wise world?

But you play like the Spider that makes her webbe to intrap and snare litle Flyes, but weaues it so slenderly, that the great ones breake through without any dammage. You straine Gnats, and passe ouer Elephants; you scoure the ponde of a fewe croakyng Frogges, and leaue behinde an infinite number of most venemous Scorpions. You decypher poore Conny-catchers, that perhaps with a tricke at cardes, winne fortie shillings from a churle that can spare it, and neuer talke of those Caterpillers that vndoo the poore, ruine whole Lordships, infect the common-wealth, and delight in nothing but in wrongfull extorting and purloyning of pelfe, when as such be the greatest Conny-catchers of all, as by your leaue maister *R. G.* I wil make manifest.

Sir reuerence on your worship, had you such a moate in your eye, that you could not see those Fox-furd Gentlemen that hyde vnder their gownes faced with foynes, more falshood then all the Conny-catchers in England beside, those miserable Vsurers (I meane) that like Vultures pray vppon the spoyle of the poore, / sleeping with his [A4ᵛ neighbors pledges all night in his bosome, and feeding vpon forfaits and penalties, as the rauens doe vppon carren? If his poore neighbor want to supply his need, eyther for his houshold necessaries, or his rent at the day, he wil not lende a peny for charitie, all his money is abroad: but if he offer him either cow or sow, mare or horse, or the very corne scarse sprowted out of the ground to sel, so the bargaine may be cheape, though to the beggery of the poore man, hee choppes with him straight, and makes the poore Conny fare the worse all the yeare after. Why write you not of these Connycatchers Maister *R. G.*?

Besides if pawnes come, as the lease of a house, or the feesimple in morgage, hee can out of his furd cassocke draw money to lend: but the olde Cole hath such quirkes and quiddities in the conueyance, such prouisoes, such dayes, howers, nay minutes of payments, that if his neighbor breake but a moment, he takes the forfayt, and like a pinke-eyed Ferret so clawes the poore Cony in the burrow, that he leaues no haire on his breach nor on his backe ere he partes with him. Are not these vipers of the commonwelth, and to be exclaimde against, not in smal Pamphlets, but in great volumes?

You set downe how there bee requisite Setters and Versers in Conny-catching, and be there not so I pray you in Vsury? for when a yoong youthful Gentleman, giuen a little to lash out liberalley, wanteth money, makes hee not his moane first to the Broker, as subtil a knaue to induce him to his ouerthrowe, as the wyliest Setter or Verser in England? and he must be feede to speake to the Vsurer, and haue so much in the pound for his labour: then he shal haue graunt of money and commodities together, so that if he borrow a hundred pound, he shal haue fortie in siluer, and threescore in wares, dead stuffe God wot; as Lute strings, Hobby horses, or (if he be greatly fauored) browne paper or cloath, and that shootes out in the lash. Then his lande is turnde ouer in statute or recognizance for sixe moneths and sixe moneths, so that he payes some thirty in the hundred to the Vsurer, beside the Scriuener he hath a blind share: but when he comes to sel his threescore pound commodities, tis wel if he get fiue and thirtie. /   [B1

Thus is the poore gentleman made a meere and simple Conny, and verst vpon to the vttermost, and yet if he breake his day, loseth as much land as cost his father a thousand markes.

Is not this coossenage and Conny-catching Maister *R G.* and more daily practised in England, and more hurtful then our poore shifting at Cardes, and yet your mashippe can winke at the cause? they be wealthy, but *Cuthbert Conny-catcher* cares for none of them no more then they care for him, and therfore wil reueale all. And because Maister *R. G.* you were pleasant in examples, Ile tel you a tale of an Vsurer, done within a mile of a knaues head, and since the Cuckow sung last, and it fell out thus.

A pleasant tale of an Vsurer.

IT fortuned that a yoong gentleman not farre off from *Cockermouth*, was somewhat slipt behind hand, and growne in debt, so that he durst hardly shew his head for feare of his creditors, and hauing wife and children to maintaine, although he had a proper land, yet wanting money to stocke his ground, he liued very bare: whereupon he determined with himselfe to goe to an olde penny-father that dwelt hard by him, and to borrow some money of him, and so to lay his land in morgage for the repayment of it.

He no sooner made the motion but it was accepted, for it was a goodly Lordship, worth in rent of assise seuen score pound by the yeare, and did abbut vpon the Vsurers ground, which drew the old churle to be maruellous willing to disburse money, so that he was content to lende him two hundred markes for three yeare according to the statute, so that he might haue the land for assurance of his money.

The gentleman agreed to that, and promised to acknowledge a statute staple to him, with letters of defeysance. The Vsurer (although he likt this wel, and saw the yong man offered more than reason required) yet had a further fetch to haue the land his whatsoeuer should chaunce, and therefore he began to verse vppon the poore Conny thus.

Sir (quoth he) if I did not pittie your estate, I would not lende you my money at such a rate: for whereas you haue it after ten / pounds in the [B1v hundred, I can make it worth thirtie. But seeing the distresse you your wife and children are in, and considering all growes through your owne liberall nature, I compassionate you the more, and would do for you as for mine owne sonne: therefore if you shal thinke good to follow it, I wil giue you fatherly aduise, I knowe you are greatly indebted, and haue many vnmercifull creditors, and they haue you in suit, and I doubt ere long wil haue some extent against your lands, so shal you be vtterly vndone, and I greatly incumbred. Therefore to auoyd all this, in my iudgement it were best for you to make a deed of gift of all your landes, without condition or promise, to some one faythful friend or other, in whom you may repose credite, so shal your enemies haue no aduauntage against you: and seeing they shall haue nothing but your bare body lyable to their executions, they wil take the more easie and speedy composition. I thinke this the surest way, and if you durst repose your selfe in me, God is my witnesse, I would be to you as your father if he liued. How say you to this compendious tale Maister *R. G.* could the proudest setter or verser in the world haue drawne on a Conny more cunningly?

Wel, againe to our yoong gentleman, who simply (with teares in his eyes to heare the kindnes of the Vsurer) thankt him hartily, and deferred not to put in practise his counsell, for he made an absolute deed of gift from wife and children to this Vsurer of all his Lordshippe, and so had the two hundred markes vpon the playne forfait of a band.

To be short, the money made him and his merry, and yet he did husband it so wel, that he not onely duly paid the interest, but stockt his grounds, and began to grow out of debt, so that his creditors were willing to beare with him. Against the three yeares were expired, he made shift by the helpe of

his friends for the money, and carryed it home to
the Vsurer, thanking him greatly, and crauing a
returne of his deed of gift. Nay soft sir (sayth the
olde Churle) that bargaine is yet to make, the land
is mine to mee and mine heyres for euer, by a deed
of gift from your owne hand, and what can be more
sure: take the money if you please, and there is
your band, but for the Lordship I wil enter on it
to morrow: yet if you wil be my tenant, you shall
haue it before another, and that is all / the [B2
fauour you shal haue of me.

At this the Gentleman was amazed, and began
to plead conscience with him, but in vaine: whereuppon he went sorrowfully home and told his wife,
who as a woman halfe lunatike ran with hir little
children to his house, and cryed out, but bootlesse:
For although they called him before the chiefe of
the country, yet sith the law had graunted him the
feesimple thereof he would not part withal: so that
this distressed gentleman was faine to become
tenant to this Vsurer, and for two hundred marks
to lose a Lordship worth six or seuen thousand
pounds. I pray you was not this an old Conycatcher
M. *R. G.* that could lurtch a poore Conny of so
many thousands at one time? whether is our cros-
sing at cardes more perillous to the commonwelth
than this cossenage for land? you winke at it, but
I wil tel all, yet heare out the end of my tale, for as

fortune fel out, the Vsurer was made a Cony himselfe.

The gentleman and his wife smothering this with patience, she that had a reaching wit, & hair brain reuenge in hir head, counseld hir husband to make a voyage from home, & to stay a weeke or two: and (q. she) before you come againe you shal see mee venter faire for the land. The gentleman willing to let his wife practise hir wits, went his way, and left al to his wiues discretion. She after hir husband was foure or fiue dayes from home, was visited by the Vsurer, who vsed hir very kindly, and sent victuals to hir house, promising to sup with hir that night, and that she should not want any thing in hir husbands absence. The gentlewoman with gratious acceptance thankt him, and bad diuers of hir neighbors to beare him company, hauing a further reatch in hir heade then he suspected. For the olde Churle comming an hower before Supper time, euen as she hir selfe would wish, for an amorous wehe or two, as olde Iades wynnie when they cannot wagge the tayle, began to be very pleasant with his tenant, and desired her to shew him al the roomes in hir house, and happily (saith he) if I die without issue, I may giue it to your children, for my conscience bids me be fauorable to you.

The gentlewoman lead him through euery part,

and at last brought him into a backe roome much like a backhouse, where she said thus vnto him./

Sir, this roome is the most vnhandsomest in [B2ᵛ] all the house, but if there were a dormar built to it, and these shut windows made bay windows and glazd, it would make the properest parlour in al the house: for (saith she) put your head out at this window, and looke what a sweet prospect belongs vnto it.

The Vsurer mistrusting nothing, thrust out his craftie sconce, and the Gentlewoman shut to the windowe, and called her maids to helpe, where they bound and pinyond the caterpillers armes fast, and then stood he with his head into a backe-yard, as if he had beene on a pillory, and struggle durst not for stifling himselfe. When she had him thus at the vauntage, she got a couple of sixe peny nayles and a hammer, and went into the yard, hauing her children attending vpon her, euery one with a sharpe knife in theyr handes, and then comming to him with a sterne countenance, shee looked as *Medea* did when she attempted reuenge against *Iason*. The Vsurer seeing this tragedie, was afraid of his life, and cryed out, but in vaine, for her maydes made such a noyse, that his shriking could not be heard, whilest she nayled one eare fast to the windowe, and the other to the stanshel, then began she to vse these words vnto him.

E

Ah vile and iniurious caterpiller, God hath sent thee to seeke thine owne reuenge, and now I and my children wil performe it. For sith thy wealth doth so countenance thee, that we cannot haue thee punisht for thy coossenage, I my selfe wil bee Iustice, Iudge, and Executioner: for as the Pillory belongs to such a villaine, so haue I nayled thy eares, and they shal be cut off to the perpetuall example of such purloining reprobates, and the executers shal bee these little infants, whose right without conscience or mercie thou so wrongfully deteinest. Looke on this old Churle litle babes, this is he that with his coossenage wil driue you to beg and want in your age, and at this instant brings your Father to all this present miserie, haue no pittie vppon him, but you two cut off his eares, and thou (quoth she to the eldest) cut off his nose, and so be reuenged on the villaine whatsoeuer fortune me for my labour. At this the Vsurer cryed out, and bad her stay her children, and hee would restore the house & land again to hir husband. I cannot beleeue thee base churle q. she, for thou that wouldst periure thy selfe/against so honest [B3 a Gentleman as my husband, wil not sticke to forsweare thy selfe were thou at liberty and therefore I wil mangle thee to the vttermost. As thus she was ready to haue her children fal vpon him, one of hir maydes came running in, and told her, her neighbors were come to supper: bid them come in, quoth she, and behold this spectacle. Although the Vsurer was passing loath to haue his neighbors see him thus tyranously vsed, yet in they came, and when they saw him thus mannerly in a new made pillory, and his eares fast nayled, some wondred, some laught, and all stood amazed, till the Gentlewoman discourst to them all the coosenage, and how she meant to be reuenged: some of them perswaded her to let him go, others were silent, and some bad him confesse: he hearing them debate the matter, and not to offer to helpe him, cryed out: why, and stand you staring on me neighbors, and wil not you saue my life? No quoth the Gentlewoman, he or she that stirs to helpe thee shal pay dearely for it, and therefore my boyes, off with his eares: then he cryed out, but stay, and he would confesse all, when from point to point he rehearst how he had coossened hir husband by a deed of gift only made to him in trust, and there was content to giue him the two hundreth markes freely for amends, and to yeeld vp before any men of worship the land againe into his possession, and vpon that he bad them all beare witnes. Then the gentlewoman let loose his eares, and let slip his head, and away went he home with his bloody lugges, and tarryed not to take part of the meat he had sent, but the gentlewoman & her neighbors made merry therwith, and laught hartily at the vsage of the vsurer. The next day it was bruted abroad, and came to the eares of the worshipful of the country, who sate in commission vppon it, and found out the coossenage of the Vsurer, so they praised the witte of the Gentlewoman, restored her husband to the land, and the old churle remained in discredit, and was a laughing stocke to all the country all his life after.

I pray you what say to Mounser the Miller with the gilden thumbe, whether thinke you him a Conny catcher or no? that robs euery poore man of his meale and corne, and takes towle at his owne pleasure, how many Conyes doth hee take vp in a yeare? for when he brings them wheat to the Mill, he sels them meale of / their owne corne in the [B3v] market. I omit *Miles* the Millers coossenage for wenching affaires, as no doubt in these causes they bee mighty Cony-catchers, and meane to speake of their pollicie in filtching and stealing of meale. For you must note, that our iolly Miller doth not only verse vpon the poore and rich for their towle, but hath false hoppers conueyed vnder the fal of his Mill, where al the best of the meale runs by, this is, if the partie be by that bringeth the corne: but because many men haue many eyes, the Miller will driue them off for their griest for a day or two, and then he playes his pranks at his owne pleasure. I need not tel that stale ieast of the Gentlemans Miller that kept Court and Leet once euery weeke, and vsed to set in euery sacke a candle, and so summon the owners to appeare by their names, if they came not, as they were farre inough from that place, then he amerced them, and so tooke treple towle of euery sacke. One night amongst the rest, the Gentleman his maister was vnder the Mill, and heard all his knauery, how euery one was called, and paid his amerciament, at last he heard his owne name called, and then stepping vp the Ladder, he bad stay, for he was there to make his appearance. I do imagine that the Miller was blanke, and perhaps his Maister called him knaue, but the Fox the more he is curst the better he fares, and the oftener the Miller is called theefe, the richer he waxeth: and therefore doe men rightly by a by word bid the Miller put out, and if he asketh what, they say a theeues head and a theeues paire of eares: for such graund Cony-catchers are these Millers, that he that cannot verse vpon a poore mans sacke, is said to be borne with a golden thumbe. But that you may see more plainly theyr knauery, Ile tel you a pleasant tale, performed not many yeares since by a Miller in *Enfield* Mil, ten miles from *London*, and an Alewiues boy of *Edmondton*, but because they are al at this present aliue, I wil conceale their names, but thus it fel out.

A pleasant Tale of a Miller and an Alewiues Boy of Edmondton.

AN Alewife of *Edmondton*, who had a great vent for spiced Cakes, sent her sonne often to *Endfield* Mill for to haue her / wheat ground, [B4 so that the Boy who was of a quicke spirit & rype wit, grew very familiar both with the Miller and his man, and could get his corne sooner put in the Mil then any Boy in the country beside. It fortuned on a time, that this good wife wanting meale, bad her Boy hie to the Mil, and be at home that night without faile, for she had not a pint of floure in the house. Iacke her sonne, for so we wil cal his name, layes his sacke on his mares backe, and away he rides singing towardes *Endfield*: as he rode, he mette at the washes with the Miller, and gaue him the time of the day, Godfather quoth he, whither ride you? to *London* Iacke quoth the Miller: Oh good Godfather quoth the boy, tel mee what store of griest is at the Mil? marry great store quoth the Miller: but Iacke if thou wilt do me an arrant to my man, ile send thee by a token that thou shalt haue thy corn cast on & ground assoone as thou commest, Ile say and doe what you wil to be dispatcht, for my mother hath neyther Cakes nor floure at home: then Iacke saith the Miller, bid my man grind thy corne next, by that token he looke to my Bitch and feed her wel. I wil Godfather saith the Boy, and rides his way, and marueiled with himself what Bitch it was that he bad his man feede, considering for two or three yeares he had vsde to the Mil, and neuer saw a Dog nor Bitch, but a little prickeard Shault that kept the Mil doore. Riding thus musing with himselfe, at last he came to *Endfield*, and there he had his corne wound vp: assoon as he came vp the stairs, the Millers man being somewhat sleepy began to aske Iack drowsily what newes. Marry quoth the Boy, the newes is this, that I must haue my corne laide on next: soft Iacke quoth the Millers man, your turne wil not come afore midnight, but ye are alwayes in hast, soft fire makes sweet mault, your betters shal be serued afore you this time. Not so quoth the Boy, for I met my Godfather at the washes riding to *London*, and tolde him what hast I had, and so he bids my griest shal be layde on next, by that token you must looke to his Bitch and feed her wel. At that the Millers man smilde, and said he should be the next, and so rose vp and turned a pinne behind the Hopper. Iacke markt al this, and beeing a wily and a witty Boy, mused where this Bitch should be, and seeing none, began to suspect some knauery, and therefore being very/ familiar, was bold to looke about in euery [B4ᵛ corner, while the man was busie about the Hopper, at last Iacke turning vp a cloath that hung before the Trough, spied vnder the Hopper belowe, where a great Poake was tyed with a cord almost ful of fine floure, that ranne at a false hole vnderneath, and could not be spyed by any meanes, Iacke seeing this, beganne to suspect this was the Millers Bitch that hee commanded his man to feede, and so smiled and let it alone: at last when the corne was ground off that was in the Hopper, Iacke layde on his, and was very busie about it himselfe, so that the Millers man set him downe and tooke a nap, knowing the Boye could looke to the mill almost as wel as himselfe, Iacke all this while had an eye to the Bitch, and determined at last to slip her haulter, which he warily performed, for when his corne was ground and he had put vp his meale, he whipst asunder the cord with his knife that held the Poake, & thrust it into the mouth of his sacke, now there was in the Poake a bushell and more of passing fine floure, that the Millers Bitch had eaten that day, assoone as Iacke had tyed vp his sacke, there was striuing who should laye on corne next, so that the Millers man wakte, and Iacke desiring one to helpe him vp with his corne, tooke his leaue and went his way, ryding merely homeward, smiling to thinke how he had cousoned the Miller, as he roade, at that same place where hee mette the Miller outward, he met him homeward, How now Iacke quoth the Miller hast ground, I, I thanke you Godfather quoth the Boy, but didst remember my arrant to my man sayes he, didst bid him looke to my Bitch wel, Oh Godfather quoth the Boy, take no care for your Bitch she is wel, for I haue her here in my sacke whelpes and all, away rydes Iacke at this laughing, and the Miller grieuing, but when he found it true, I leaue you to gesse how hee and his man dealt togither, but how the Alewife sported at the knauery of her sonne when he told her all the ieast, that imagine, but how soeuer for all that, Iack was euer welcome to the Mill and ground before any, and whose soeuer sacke fedde the Bitch, Iackes scapte euer towle-free, that hee might conceale the Millers subtiltie.

Was not this Miller a Conny-catcher maister *R. G* ? What should I talke of the baser sort of men, whose occupation cannot bee vpholden without craft, there is no mysterie nor science almost, wherin a man may thriue, without it be lincked to this famous Art of Conny-catching. The Alewife vnles she nicke her Pots and Conny-catch / her [C1 guestes with stone Pottes and petty Cannes, can hardly paye her Brewer, nay and yet that wil not serue, the chalke must walke to set vp now & then a shilling or two too much, or else the rent wil not bee answered at the quarter day, besides ostrey, faggots, and faire chambring, and pretty wenches that haue no wages, but what they get by making of beddes. I know some Taphouses about the Subberbes, where they buy a shoulder of mutton for two groats, and sel it to their ghuest for two shillings, and yet haue no female friends to sup withall, let such take heed, least my fathers white Horse loose saddle & bridle & they go on foote to the diuel on pilgrimage. Tush maister *R. G.* God is my witnesse, I haue seene Chaunlers about *London*, haue two paire of waites, and when the searchers come, they shewe them those that are sealed, but when their poore neighbors buy ware, they vse them that lack weight, I condemne not all, but let such amend as are toucht at the quick. And is not this flat Conny-catching, yes, if it please your maship & worser. Why the base sort of Ostlers haue their shifts, & the crue of S Patrickes Costerdmongers, can sell a simple man a crab for a pipping. And but that I haue loued wine wel, I wold touch both the Vintner and his bush, for they haue such brewing and tunning, such chopping and changing, such mingling & mixing, what of wine with water in the quart pot, and tempering one wine with another in the vessel, that it is hard to get a neate cup of wine and simple of it selfe, in most of our ordinary Tauerns, & do not they make poore men connies, that for their currant mony giue them counterfeit wine.

What say you to the Butcher with his prickes, that hath pollicies to puffe vp his meate to please the eye, is not al his craft vsed to draw the poore Conny to ryd him of his ware. Hath not the Draper his darke shop to shadow the dye and wooll of his cloth, and all to make the country Gentleman or Farmer a conny. What trade can maintaine his traffique? what science vphold it self? what man liue, vnles he growe into the nature of a Cony-catcher? Doo not the Lawyers make long Pleaes, stand vpon their demurres, and haue their quirks and quiddities to make his poore Client a Cony? I speake not generally, for so they be the ministers of iustice, and the Patrons of the poore mens right, but particularly of such as hold gaines their God, and esteeme more of coyne then of conscience. I remember by the way a merry iest performed by a Foole, yet wittily hit home at hazard, as blinde men shoote the Crow. /   [C1ᵛ

A pleasant Tale of Will Sommers.

King *Henry* the eight of famous memory, walking one day in his priuy Garden, with *Will Sommers* his Foole, it fortuned that two Lawyers had a suite vnto his maiestie for one piece of grounde that was almost out of lease and in the Kinges gift, and at time put vp their Supplication to his highnesse, and at that instant one of the Pantry that had been a long seruiture, had spyed out the same land, and exhibited his petition for the same gift, so that in one houre, all the three Supplications were giuen to the King, which his highnesse noting, and being as then pleasantly disposed, he reuealed it to them that were by him, how there were three Fishes at one bayte, and all gapte for a benefice, and hee stood in doubt on whome to bestowe it, and so shewed them the Supplications, the Courtiers spoke for their felow, except two that were feed by the Lawyers, and they particularly pleaded for their friendes, yelding many reasons to the King on both sides. At last his maiestie sayd, hee would referre the matter to *Will Sommers*, which of them his Foole thought most worthy of it should haue the lande. *Will* was glad of this, and loued him of the Pantrie wel, and resolued he should haue the ground, but the Foole brought it about with pretty iest, Marry quoth he, what are these two Lawiers? I *Will* saide the King, then quoth the Foole, I wil vse them as they vse their poore clients. Looke here quoth he, I haue a Walnut in my hand, and I wil diuide it among the three, so *Will* crackt it, and gaue to one Lawyer one shel, and to an other the other shel, and to him of the Pantry the meat, so shal thy gift be *Harry*, quoth he, this Lawyer shal haue good Bookes, and this faire promises, but my felow of the Pantry shal haue the land. For thus deale they with their clyents, two men goe to two, and spende all that they haue vpon the Lawe, and at last, haue nothing but bare shales for their labour. At this, the King and his Noble men laught: the Yeoman of the Pantry had the gift, and the Lawyers went home with fleas in their eares, by a Fooles verdite. I rehearst this Act to shew how men of Lawe, feede on poore mens purses, and makes their country clyents, oftentimes simple connyes. But leauing these common courses and triuial examples, I will shew you maister *R. G.* of a kinde of *Conny-catchers*, that as yet passeth al these.

There bee in *Englande*, but especially about *London*, certayne quaint, pickt, and neate companions, attyred in their apparel, eyther / *alla mode de Fraunce*, with a side Cloake, and a hat of a high blocke and a broad brimme, as if hee could with his head cosmographise the world in a moment, or else *Allespanyole*, with a straight bombaste sleeue like a quaile pipe, his short Cloake, and his Rapier hanging as if he were entering the List to a desperate Combate: his beard squared with such Art, eyther with his mustachies after the lash of Lions, standing as stiffe as if he wore a Ruler in his mouth, or else nickt off with the *Italian* cut, as if he ment to professe one faith with the vpper lippe, and an other with his nether lippe, and then hee must be Marquisadod, with a side peake pendent, eyther sharpe lyke the single of a Deere, or curtold lyke the broad ende of a Moule spade. This Gentleman forsooth, hanteth Tabling houses, Tauerns, and such places, where yong nouices resort, & can fit his humor to all companies, and openly shadoweth his disguise with the name of a Traueller, so that he wil haue a superficiall insight into certaine phrases of euerie language, and pronounce them in such a grace, as if almost hee were that Countryman borne: then shal you heare him vaunt of his trauels, and tel what wonders he hath seene in strange countries: how he hath bin at Saint *Iames* of *Compostella* in *Spaine*, at *Madril* in the Kings Court: and then drawing out his blade, hee claps it on the boord, and sweares he bought that in *Toledo*: then wil he roue to *Venice*, and with a sigh, discouer the situation of the citie, how it is seated two Leagues from *Terra frenia*, in the Sea, and speake of *Rialto Treuiso* and *Murano*, where they make Glasses: and to set the young gẽtlemans teeth an edge, he wil make a long tale of *La Strado Courtizano*, wher the beautiful Curtizans dwel, discribing their excellency, and what angellical creatures they be, and how amorously they wil entertaine strangers. Tush, he wil discourse the state of *Barbary*, and there to *Eschites* and

Alcaires, and from thence leape to *Fraunce*, *Denmarke*, and *Germany*, After all concluding thus.

What is a Gentleman (saith he) without trauaile? euen as a man without one eye. The sight of sundry countries made *Vlisses* so famous: bought witte is the sweetest, and experience goeth beyond all Patrymonies. Did young Gentlemen, as wel as I, know the pleasure & profit of trauel, they would not keep them at home within their natiue continent: but visit the world, & win more wisedome in trauelling two or three yeeres, then all the wealth their Ancestors left them to possesse. Ah the sweet sight of ladies, the strange wonders in cities, / [C2ᵛ and the diuers manners of men and theyr conditions, were able to rauish a yong Gentlemans sences with the surfet of content, and what is a thousand pound spent to the obtaining of those pleasures.

All these Nouelties doth this pipned Bragout boast on, when his only trauaile hath been to look on a faire day, from *Douer Clifts* to *Callis*, neuer hauing stept a foot out of *England*, but surueyed the Maps, and heard others talke what they knew by experience. Thus decking himselfe like the Daw with the faire feathers of other birds, and discoursing what he heard other men report, hee grew so plausible among yoong Gentlemen, that he got his Ordinary at the least, and some gratious thanks for his labour. But happily some amongst many, tickled with the desire to see strange countries, and drawne on by his alluring words, would ioyne with him, and question if he meant euer to trauaile againe. He straight after he hath bitten his peake by the end, *Alla Neopolitano* begins thus to reply.

Sir, although a man of my trauel and experience might be satisfied in the sight of countries, yet so insaciat is the desire of trauailing, that if perhaps a yong Gentleman of a liberal and courteous nature, were desirous to see *Ierusalem* or *Constantinople*, would he wel acquit my paines and followe my counsaile, I would bestow a yeare or two with him out of England. To be breefe, if the Gentleman iumpe with him, then doth he cause him to sel some Lordship, and put some thousand or two thousand pound in the banke to be receyued by letters of exchange: and because the gentleman is ignorant, my yong Maister his guide must haue the disposing of it: which he so wel sets out, that the poore gentleman neuer sees any returne of his mony after. Then must store of suites of apparel be bought and furnisht euery way: at last, he names a ship wherein they should passe, and so downe to *Grauesend* they go, and there he leaues the yoong nouice, fleest of his money and wo begone, as farre from trauaile as *Miles* the merry Cobler of *Shorditch*, that swore he would neuer trauaile further,

CONNY-CATCHING

than from his shop to the Alehouse. I pray you cal you not these fine witted fellowes *Conny-catchers* Maister *R. G.*?

But now Sir by your leaue a little, what if I should proue you a *Conny-catcher* Maister *R. G.* would it not make you blush at the matter? Ile go as neare to it as the Fryer did to his Hostesse mayde, when the Clarke of the parish tooke him at *Leuatem* at midnight. Aske the Queens Players, if you sold them not *Orlando Furioso* / for twenty Nobles, and when they were in the country, sold the same Play to the Lord Admirals men for as much more. Was not this plaine *Conny-catching* Maister *R. G*?

But I heare when this was obiected, that you made this excuse: that there was no more faith to be held with Plaiers, than with them that valued faith at the price of a feather: for as they were *Comædians* to act, so the actions of their liues were *Cameleon* like, that they were vncertaine, variable, time pleasers, men that measured honestie by profite, and that regarded their Authors not by desart, but by necessitie of time. If this may serue you for a shadow, let mee vse it for an excuse of our Card *Conny-catching*: for when we meet a country Farmar with a ful purse, a miserable miser, that eyther rackes his Tenants rents, or selles his graine in the market at an vnreasonable rate: we hold it a deuotion to make him a Conny, in that he is a Caterpiller to others, and gets that by pilling and polling of the poore, that we strip him of by sleight and agilitie of wit.

Is there not heere resident about London, a crew of terryble Hacksters in the habite of Gentlemen, wel appareld, and yet some weare bootes for want of stockings, with a locke worne at theyr lefte eare for their mistrisse fauour, his Rapyer *Alla reuolto*, his Poynado pendent ready for the stab, and *cauileuarst* like a warlike *Magnifico*: yet for all this outward shew of pride, inwardly they be humble in minde, and despise worldly welth, for you shal neuer take them with a penny in theyr purse. These *Souldados*, for vnder that profession most of them wander, haue a pollicie to scourge Alehouses, for where they light in, they neuer leape out, till they haue shewed theyr Arithmatike with chalke on euery post in the house, figured in Cyphers like round Os, till they make the goodman cry O, O, O, as if hee should cal an O yes at Size or Sessions. Now sir, they haue sundry shifts to maintaine them in this versing, for eyther they creep in with the goodwife, and so vndoo the goodman, or els they beare it out with great brags if the Host be simple, or els they trip him in some wordes when he is tipsy, that he hath spoken against some Iustice of peace or other, or some other great man: and then they hold him at a bay with that, til his backe almost breake. Thus shift they from house to house, hauing this prouerbe amongst them: *Such must eate as are hungry and they must pay that haue money.* Call you not these *Conny-catchers* Maister R. G.? /

It were an endlesse peece of work, to discouer the abhominable life of brokers, whose shops are the very temples of the deuil, themselues his priests, and their books of account more damnable, than the *Alcoran* set out by *Mahomet*: for as they induce yoong gentlemen to pawne their lands, as I said before: so they are ready (the more is the pitty that it is suffered) to receiue any goods, howsoeuer it bee come by, hauing their shoppes, (as they say) a lawful market to buy and sel in, so that whence growes so many Lifts about *London*, but in that they haue Brokers their friends, to buy whatsoeuer they purloyne & steale? And yet is the Picklocke, Lift, or Hooker, that brings ye stolne goods, made a flat Conny, and vsed as an Instrument onely of theyr villany: for suppose he hath lifted a gowne or a cloake, or so many parcels as are worth tenne pounds, and venters his life in hazard for the obtaining of it: the miserable Caterpiller the Broker, wil thinke hee dealeth liberally with him if he giue him forty shillings, so doth he not onely maintaine fellony, but like a theefe coossens the theefe. And are not these graund *Conny-catchers* Maister *R. G.*?

I knew not farre from Fleetbridge a Haberdasher, it were a good deed to take *Paine* to tel his name, that tooke of a boy of seuen yeere old a Rapier worth forty shillinges, and a stitch taffata Hat woorth ten, and all for fiue shillings: the Gentleman, father to the child, was sicke when necessitie droue him thus nigh, to lay his weapon and his Bonnet to pawne, and assoone as he recouered, which was within sixe weeks after, sent the money and twelue pence for the lone, to haue the parcels againe. But this Cutthrotes answer was, the Boy had made him a bil of sale of his hand for a moneth, and the day was broken, and he had made the best of the Rapier and Hat. Was not this a *Iewe* and a notable *Conny-catcher* Maister *R. G.*

It had beene wel if you had rould out your Rhetorike against such a rakehel. But come to theyr honest kinde of life, and you shal see how they stand vpon circumstances: if you borrow but two shillings, there must be a groat for the money, and a groat for the Bil of sale, and this must bee renewed euery moneth: so that they resemble the Boxe at dice, which beeing wel payd all night, will in the morning be the greatest winner.

Wert not a merry ieast to haue a bout againe Maister *R. G.* with your poetical Brethren:

amongst the which, one learned Hypocrite, that could brooke no abuses in the Commonwealth, was so zealous, / that he began to put an English [C4 she Saint in the Legend, for the holinesse of her life: and forgot not so much as her dogge, as Tobies was remembred, that wagged his tayle at the sight of his olde Mistresse. This pure Martinist (if he were not worse) had a combat betweene the flesh and the spirite, that he must needes haue a Wife, which he cunningly conny-catcht in this manner.

A pleasant Tale how a holy brother Conny-catcht for a Wife.

FIrst you must vnderstand, that he was a kind of Scholastical panyon, nourst vp onely at Grammer schoole, least going to the Vniuersitie, through his nimble witte, too much learning should make him mad. So he had past *As in præsenti*, and was gone a proficient as farre as *Carmen Heroicum*: for he pronounst his wordes like a bragout, and helde vp his head like a Malt-horse, and could talke against Bishops, and wish very mannerly the discipline of the Primitiue Church were restored. Now sir, this Gentleman had espyed (I dare not say about Fleetstreet) a proper mayd, who had giuen hir by the decease of her

Father foure hundred pound in money, besides certaine faire houses in the Cittie: to this girle goeth this proper Greek a wooing, naming himselfe to be a Gentleman of *Cheshire*, and only sonne and heyre to his Father, who was a man of great reuenewes: and to make the matter more plausible, he had attyred his owne brother very orderly in a blew coat, and made him his seruingman, who, though he were eldest, yet to aduaunce his yonger brother to so good a marriage, was content to lie, cog, and flatter, and to take any seruile paines, to sooth vp the matter: insomuch that when her Father in law (for hir mother was marryed againe, to an honest, vertuous, and substantial man in Fleetstreet or there abouts) heard how this yoong Gentleman was a Suiter to his daughter in law, careful she shoulde doe wel, calde the Seruingman aside, which by his outward behauiour seemed to be an honest and discreet man, and began to question with him what his Maister was, of what parentage, of what possibilitie of liuing after his Fathers decease, and how many children he had beside him.

This fellow wel instructed by his holy Brother, without distrust to the man, simply as he thought, said, that he was the sonne and heire / of one [C4v] Maister &c. dwelling in Cheshire, at the Manor of &c. and that he had a yoonger brother, but this was heyre to all, and rehearst a proper liuing of some fiue hundred markes a yeare. The honest man, knowing diuers Cheshire Gentlemen of that name, gaue credyte to the fellowe, and made no further inquiry, but gaue countenaunce to my yoong Maister, who by his flattering speeches had wonne, not onely the Maydes fauour vnto the full, but also the good wil of her Mother, so that the match shortly was made vp, and marryed they shoulde bee forsooth, and then should she, her Father and her Mother, ryde home to his Father in Cheshire, to haue sufficient dowry appointed.

To bee breefe, wedded they were, and bedded they had been three or foure nights, and yet for all this fayre shew the Father was a little iealous, and smoakt him, but durst say nothing. But at last, after the marriage had beene past ouer three or foure dayes, it chaunced that her Father and this Seruingman went abroad, and past through S. Paules Churchyard amongst the Stationers, a Prentise amongst the rest, that was a Cheshire man, and knew this counterfayte Seruingman and his brother, as being borne in the same Parish where his Father dwelt, called to him, and sayde: What I, how doth your Brother *P.* how doth your Father, liues he stil? The fellow aunswered him all were wel, and loth his brothers wiues father should heare any thing, made no stay but departed.

This acquaintance naming the fellow by his name and asking for his brother, droue the honest Cittizen into a great maze, and doubted he, his wife & his daughter were made Connyes. Wel, he smoothed all vp, as if he had heard nothing, and let it passe til he had sent the man about necessary businesse, and then secretly returned againe vnto the Stacioners shop, and began to question with the Boy, if he knew the Seruingman wel, that he cald to him of late. I marry doe I sir quoth he, I know both him and his brother *P*. I can tel you they haue an honest poore man to their father, and though now in his olde age he bee scarse able to liue without the helpe of the Parish, yet he is wel beloud of all his neighbors. The man hearing this, although it greeued him that he was thus cossoned by a pallyard, yet seeing no meanes to amend it, he thought to gird his son pleasantly, & therfore bad diuers of his friends and honest wealthy neighbors to a Supper: Wel, they being at the time appoynted come, all welcome, who must sit / at [Dɪ the boordes end but my yoong Maister, and he very coyly, badde them all welcome to his fathers house, they all gaue him reuerent thankes, esteeming him to be a man of worship and worth. Assoone as all were set, and the meate serued in, and the Gentlemans Seruingman stood mannerly wayting on his brothers trencher, at last the good man of the house smiling said: Sonne *P.* I pray you let your man sit downe, and eate such part with vs as God hath sent vs. Marry quoth Maister *P.* that were wel to make my man my companion, he is wel inough, let him suppe with his fellowes. Why sir sayth he, in fayth be plaine, cal him brother, and bid him sitte downe. Come coossen *I.* quoth he, make not straunge, I am sure your brother *P.* wil giue you leaue. At this Maister *P.* blusht, and askt his Father in lawe what he meant by those wordes? and whether he thought his man his brother or no? I by my faith doe I sonne quoth he, and account thee no honest man that wilt deny thine owne brother and thy father: For sir know I haue learnd your pettegree. Alas daughter quoth he, you are wel marryed, for his Father liues of the almes of the Parish, and this poore Fellowe which he hath made his slaue, is his eldest Brother. At this his wife began to weepe, all was dasht, and what she thought God knowes. Her mother cryed out, but all was bootlesse, Maister *P.* confest the trueth, and his brother sate downe at supper, and for al that he had the wench. I pray you was not this a *Conny-catcher* Maister *R. G.*?

But now to be a little pleasant with you, let me haue your opinion what you deeme of those *Amarosos* here in England, & about London, that (because the old prouerbe saith, change of pasture makes fat calues), wil haue in euery shire in England a sundry wife, as for an instance your countryman *R. B.* are not they right *Conny-catchers*? enter into the nature of them, and see whether your pen had been better imployed in discouering their villainies, thã a simple legerdemain at cards. For suppose a man hath but one daughter, and hath no other dowrie but her beautie and honestie, what a spoile is it for hir to light in the hands of such an adulterous and incestuous rascal? had not hir father beene better to haue lost forty shillings at cardes, then to haue his daughter so connycatcht and spoyld for euer after? These youths are proper fellows, neuer without good apparel and store of crowns, wel horst, and of so quaint & fine behauior, & so eloquent, that they are able to induce a yong girle to folly, especially since they shadow theyr / villainy with the honest pretence of [D1ᵛ marriage: for theyr custome is this. When they come into the Cittie or other place of credit, or somtime in a country village, as the fortune of theyr villany leads them, they make inquiry what good marriages are abroad, & on the sunday make suruey what faire and beautiful mayds or widowes are in the Parish: then as their licentious lust leades them, whether the eye for fauour, or the eare for riches, so they set downe theyr rest, & soiourne eyther there or thereabouts, hauing money at wil,

and their companions to sooth vp whatsoeuer
damnably they shal protest, courting the maid or
widow with such faire words, & sweet promises,
that shee is often so set on fire, that neither the
report of others, nor the admonition of their frends,
can draw them from the loue of the *Poligamoi* or
bel-swaggers of the country. And when the
wretches haue by the space of a moneth or two
satisfied their lust, they waxe weary, & either faine
some great iourney for a while to be absent, & so
go & visit some other of his wiues, or els if he
meane to giue her the bagge, he selleth whatsoeuer
he can, and so leaues hir spoild both of hir wealth
and honestie, then which there is nothing more
pretious to an honest woman. And because you
shal see an instance, I wil tel you a pleasant tale
performd by our villaines in Wiltshire not long
since, I wil conceale the parties names, because I
thinke the woman is yet aliue.

*A pleasaunt Tale of a man that was marryed to
   sixteene Wiues, and how courteously his last
   wife intreated him.*

IN Wiltshire there dwelt a Farmar of indifferent
wealth, that had but onely one childe, and that
was a daughter, a mayd of excellent beauty and
good behauior, and so honest in hir conuersation,

that the good report of hir vertues was wel spoken of in all the cuntry, so that what for hir good qualities, & sufficient dowry that was like to fal to her, she had many suters, mens sons of good welth and honest conuersation. But whether this mayd had no minde to wed, or she likte none that made loue to her, or she was afrayde to match in haste least shee might repent at leysure, I know not: but she refused all, & kept her stil a virgin. But as we see oftentimes, the coyest maydes happen on the coldest mariages, playing like the beetle that makes scorne al day of the daintiest flowers, and at night takes vp his lodging in a cowsherd. So this maid, whom we wil cal *Marian*, refused many honest / and wealthy Farmars sonnes, [D2 and at last lighted on a match, that for euer after mard her market: for it fel out thus. One of these notable roges, by occupation a taylor, and a fine workman, a reprobate giuen ouer to the spoyle of honest maids, & to the deflowring of virgins, hearing as he trauelled abroad of this *Marian*, did meane to haue a fling at her, and therefore came into the towne where hir father dwelt and asked worke. A very honest man of that trade, seeing him a passing proper man, and of a very good and honest countenance, and not simply apparelled, sayd he would make trial of him for a garment or two, and so tooke him into seruice: assoone as hee saw him vse his needle, he wondered not onely at his workemanshippe, but at the swiftnes of his hand. At last the fellow (whom we wil name *William*) desired his Maister that he might vse his sheeres but once for the cutting out of a dublet, which his Maister graunted, and he vsed so excellently wel, that although his Maister was counted the best taylor in Wiltshire, yet he found himself a botcher in respect of his new intertained iourneyman, so that from that time forward he was made foreman of the shop, & so pleased the gentlemen of that shire, that who but *William* talkt on for a good taylor in that shire. Wel, as yong men and maydes meet on sondayes & holydaies, so this taylor was passing braue, & began to frolike it amongst the maydes, & to be very liberal, being ful of siluer and gold, & for his personage a properer man than any was in all the Parish, and made a far off a kind of loue to this *Marian*, who seeing this *William* to be a very handsome man, began somewhat to affect him, so that in short time she thought wel of his fauors, & there grew some loue betweene them, insomuch that it came to hir fathers eares, who began to schoole his daughter for such foolish affectiõ towards one she knew not what he was, nor whither he would: but in vaine, *Marian* could not but thinke wel of him, so that her father one day sent for his Maister, and began

to question of the disposition of his man. The
Maister told the Farmar friendly that what he was
hee knew not, as being a meere stranger vnto him:
but for his workmanship, he was one of the most
excellent both for needle and sheeres in England:
for his behauior since he came into his house, he
had behaued himself very honestly and curteously:
wel apparelled he was, and well monied, & might
for his good qualities seeme to be a good womans
fellow. Although this somewhat satisfied the
father, yet he was loth a tailor should cary away
his daughter, & that she should be driuẽ to liue /
of a bare occupation, whereas she might haue [D2ᵛ
landed men to her husbandes, so that hee and her
friendes called her aside, and perswaded her from
him, but she flatly told them she neuer loued any
but him, and sith it was her first loue, she would
not now be turned from it, whatsoeuer hap did
afterward befal vnto her. Her father that loued
her dearly, seeing no perswasions could draw her
from the taylor, left her to her owne libertie, and
so shee and *William* agreed togither, that in short
time they were married, and had a good portion,
and set vp shop, and liued togither by the space of
a quarter of a yeare very orderly. At last satisfied
with the lust of his new wife, he thought it good to
visit some other of his wiues (for at that instant hee
had sixteene aliue) and made a scuse to his wife and

CONNY-CATCHING

his wiues father to go into Yorkshire (which was his natiue country) and visit his friends, and craue somwhat of his father towards houshold. Although his wife was loth to part from her sweet *Wil.* yet she must be content, and so wel horst and prouided, away hee rydes for a moneth or two, that was his furthest day, and downe goes he into some other country to solace himself with some other of his wiues. In this meane while one of his wiues that he married in or about Tanton in Sommersetshire, had learnd of his villany, and how many wiues he had, and by long traueyle had got a note of their names and dwelling, and the hands and seales of euerie parish where he was married, and now by fortune shee heard that hee had married a wife in Wilshire, not farre from Malborough: thither hies shee with warrants from the Bishop and diuers Iustices to apprehend him, and comming to the Towne where he dwelt, verie subtilly inquired at her host of his estate, who told her that he had married a rich Farmers daughter, but now was gone downe to his friendes in Yorkshire, and would be at home againe within a weeke, for hee had been eight weekes alreadie from home. The woman inquired no further for that time, but the next morning went home to the Farmers house, and desired him to sende for his daughter, for shee would speake with her from her husband: the man

straight did so, and shee hearing she should haue
newes from her *William*, came very hastily. Then
the woman said, shee was sory for her, in that their
misfortunes were alyke, in being married to such
a runnagate as this Taylor: for (quoth shee) it is
not yet a yeare and a halfe since hee was married to
me in Somersetshire. As this went colde to the
olde mans heart, so stroke it deadly into the mind
of *Marian*, who desiring her to tell the / truth, [D3
she out with her testimony, and shewed them how
he had at that instant sixteene wiues aliue. When
they read the certificate, and sawe the handes and
seales of euery parish, the old man fel a weeping:
but such was the griefe of *Marian*, that her sorrow
stopt her teares, and she sat as a woman in a trance,
til at last fetching a great sigh, she called God to
witnes she would be reuenged on him for al his
wiues, and would make him a general example of
al such gracelesse runnagates. So she conceald the
matter, and placed this her fellow in misfortune in
a kinswomans house of hers, so secretly as might
be, attending the comming of hir trecherous husband, who returned within a fortnight, hauing in
the space hee was absent visited three or foure of
his wiues, and now ment to make a short cut of the
matter, & sel al that his new wife had, and to
trauel into some other shire, for hee had heard how
his Somersetshire wife had made inquiry after him

CONNY-CATCHING

in diuers places. Being come home he was wonderfully welcome to *Marian*, who entertained him with such curtesies as a kind wife could any waies affoord him, only y̅e vse of her body she denied, saying her natural disease was vpon her. Wel to be briefe, a great supper was made, and al her friends was bidden, & he euery way so welcome as if it had bin the day of his bridal, yea al things was smoothed vp so cunningly, y̅t he suspected nothing lesse then y̅e reuenge intēded against him. Assoone as supper was ended, & al had taken their leaue, our taylor would to bed, and his wife with her own hands helpt to vndresse him very louingly, and being laid down she kist him, & said she would go to hir fathers & come again straight, bidding him fal a sleep the whilest: hee y̅t was drowsie with trauel & drinking at supper, had no need of great intreaty, for he straight fel into a sound slumber, the whilest she had sent for his other wife, & other her neighbors disguised, & comming softly into the parlour where he lay, she turnd vp his clothes at his feete, & tyed his legs fast togither with a rope, then waking him, she asked him what reason he had to sleep so soundly. He new wakte out his sleep began to stretch himselfe, and gald his legs with the cord, whereat he wondring sayd; How now wife? whats that hurts my legs? what are my feet bound togither? *Marian* looking on him with lookes ful of death, made him this answer: I villaine, thy legs are bound, but hadst thou thy iust desart, thy necke had long since been stretcht at the gallowes, but before thou and I part, I wil make thee a iust spectacle vnto the world, for thy abhominable trechery: and with that she clapt her hand fast on the / haire of his head, and held [D3ᵛ] him down to the pillow. *William* driuen into a wondrous amaze at these words, said trembling: Sweete wife, what sodain alteration is this? what meane these words wife? Traytor (q. shee) I am none of thy wife, neither is this thy wife, & with that she brought her forth that he was maried in Somersetshire, although thou art maried to her as wel as to me, and hast like a villaine sought the spoile of fifteene women beside my selfe, & that thou shalt heare by iust certificat, & with yᵗ there was read the bedrol of his wiues, where hee married them, and where they dwelt. At this hee lay mute as in a traunce, & only for answer held vp his hands, and desired them both to be merciful vnto him, for he confest al was truth, that he had bin a hainous offender, and deserued death. Tush saith *Marian*, but how canst thou make any one of vs amends? If a man kil the father, he may satisfie the blood in the sonne: if a man steale, he may make restitution: but he that robs a woman of her honesty & virginitie, can neuer make any satisfaction:

CONNY-CATCHING

and therfore for al the rest I wil be reuenged. With that his other wife and the women clapt hold on him, & held him fast, while *Marian* with a sharpe rasor cut off his stones, and made him a gelding. I thinke shee had litle respect where the signe was, or obserued litle art for the string, but off they went, & then she cast them in his face, & said, Now lustful whoremaister, go & deceiue other women as thou hast done vs, if thou canst, so they sent in a surgion to him y^t they had prouided, & away they went. The man lying in great paine of body, & agony of mind, the surgion looking to his wound, had much ado to stanch the blood, & alwaies he laught hartily when hee thought on the reuenge, and bad a vengeance on such sow-gelders as made such large slits: but at last he laid a bloodplaister to him, & stopt his bleeding, and to be briefe, in time heald him, but with much paine. Assoone as he was whole, and might go abroad without danger, he was committed to the gaole, and after some other punishment, banished out of Wilshire and Somersetshire for euer after. Thus was this lustie cocke of the game made a capon, and as I heard, had litle lust to marry any more wiues to his dying day.

How like you of this conny-catching M. *R. G*? But because now we haue entred talke of Taylors, let mee haue a bout with them, for they bee mightie Conny-catchers in sundry kindes. I pray you what Poet hath so many fictions, what Painter so many fancies, as a Taylor hath fashions, to shew the varietie of his art? changing euery week / [D4 the shape of his apparrel into new forms, or els he is counted a meere botcher. The venetian and the gallogascaine is stale, and trunke slop out of vse, the rounde hose bumbasted close to the breech, and ruft aboue the necke with a curle, is now common to euery cullion in the country, & dublets be they neuer so quaintly quilted, yet forsooth the swaine at plough must haue his belly as side as the courtier, that hee may pisse out at a button hole at the least. And al these strange deuises doth the Taylor inuent to make poore gentlemen connies: for if they were tyed to one fashion, then stil might they know how much veluet to send to the Taylor, and then would his filching abate. But to preuent them, if he haue a french belly, he wil haue a Spanish skirt, and an Italian wing, seamed and quartered at the elbows, as if he were a souldado readye to put on an armour of proofe to fight in Mile-ende vnder the bloudy ensigne of the Duke of Shorditch. Thus wil the fantasticke Taylor make poore gentlemen Conies, & euer aske more veluet by a yarde and a halfe then the doublet in conscience requires. But herein lies the least part of their cony-catching: for those graund Taylors that haue al the right properties of the mysterie, which is to be knauish, theeuish, and proude, take this course with courtiers and courtly gentlemen, they finde outside, inside, lace, drawing out, and making, and then set downe their parcels in a bil, which they so ouerprise, that some of them with very pricking vp of dublets, haue fleest yong gentlemen of whole Lordships, & cal you not this cony-catching M. *R. G*? To vse the figure *Pleonasmos, Hisce oculis,* with these eies I haue seene Taylors prentises sel as much vales in a weeke in cloth of golde, veluet, satten, taffata, and lace, as hath beene woorth thirtie shillinges, and these eares hath heard them scorne when their vales came but to ten shillinges, and yet there were foure prentises in the shop. If the prentises could lurch so mightily, then what did the maister? But you must imagine this was a womans taylor, that could in a gowne put seuenteene yards of ell broad taffata, blest be the French sleeues & breech verdingales, that grants them liberty to conny-catch so mightily. But this I talke of our London and courtly Taylors: but euen the poore pricklouse the country taylor, that hath scarse any more wealth then his thimble, his needle, his pressing yron, and his sheers, wil filtch as wel as the proudest of that trade in England, they wil to snip and snap, that al the reuersion goes into hel. Now sir, this hel is a place that the tailors haue vnder their shopboord, wher al their / stolne shreds is thrust, and I [D4v] pray you cal you not this pilling & polling, and flat Conny-catching Maister *R. G*? But because you may see whether I speake truth or no, Ile tel you a merry iest of a Taylor in Yorke not farre from Petergate, done about fourteene yeare ago, and thus it fel out.

A pleasant Tale of a Taylor, how he conny-catcht a Gentlewoman, and was made himselfe a Conny afterwardes by his man.

IN Yorkeshire there dwelt a womans Taylor famous for his Art, but noted for his filching, which although hee was light fingerd, yet for the excellency of his workmanship, hee was much sought too, and kept more Iournymen, then any fiue in that citie did: and albeit hee would haue his share of veluet, satten, or cloth of golde, yet they must find no fault with him, least he half spoyld their garment in ye making. Besides, he was passing proud, and had as haughtie a looke, as if his father had with the diuel lookte ouer Lyncolne: his ordinary dublets were Taffata cut in the sommer vpon a wrought shirt, and his cloake faced with veluet, his stockinges of the purest granado silke, with a French painde hoase of the richest

billiment lace, a beauer hatte turft with veluet, so
quaintly as if he had been some Espagnolo trickt
vp to goe court some quaint curtesine, insomuch
that a plaine seruingman once meeting him in this
attire, going through Waingat to take aire in the
field, thought him at the least some Esquire, and
of with his Hat and gaue his worship the time of
the day, this clawed this *Glorioso* by the elbow, so
that if a Tauerne had been by, a pottle of wine
should haue been the least reward for a largesse to
the simple seruing man: but this bowical huffe
snuffe, not content to passe away with one worship,
began to hold the fellow in prate, and to question
whose man hee was. The felow curteously making
a low cringe saide, may it please your woorship, I
serue such a Gentleman dwelling in such a place,
as thus he answered him, he spied in the gentlemans bosome a needle and a threed, whereupon
the felow simply sayd to him, fie your woorships
man in looking this morning to your doublet, hath
left a needle and a threede on your worships brest,
you had best take it off, least some thinke your
worship to bee a Taylour. The Taylour not
thinkyng the felow had spoken simply, but frumpt
him, made this reply: what / sawcy knaue doest [E1
thou mocke mee? what if I bee a taylour, whats
that to thee, wert not for shame I would lende thee
a boxe on the eare or two, the felow being plaine,

but peeuish and an olde knaue, gathering by his owne words that he was a taylour, sayd, fye so God helpe me I mocke you not, but are you a taylour, I marry am I quoth he, why then sayes the seruyng man, all my cappes, knees, and worships, I did to thy apparrel, and therefore maister thanke mee, for it twas agaynst my wil, but now I knowe thee farewel good honest prickelouce, and looke not behynde you, for if you doo, ile swindge you in my scabberd of my sword til I can stand ouer thee, away went *Monsier Magnifico* frowning, and the seruyng man went into the Citie laughing: but all this is but to describe the nature of the man, now to the secretes of his Art, all the Gentlewomen of the Countrey cryde out vpon him, yet could they not part from him, because he so quaintly fitted their humors, at last it so fel out, that a Gentlewoman not farre from *Feroy Brigges*, had a taffata gowne to make, and hee would haue no lesse at those dayes then eleuen els of elbroad taffata, so shee bought so much and readie to send it, shee sayd to her husband in hearing of al her seruingmen, what a spight is this, seeing that I must send alwayes to yonder knaue taylor two yards more then is necessary, but how can we amend vs, all the rest are but botchers in respect of him, and yet nothing grieues mee but we can neuer take him with it, & yet I and mine haue stood by while hee

hath cut my gowne out, a pleasant fellowe that was
new come to serue her husband, one that was his
Clarke and a prety scholer, answered good mistris
giue me leaue to carry your taffata and see it cut
out, and if I spy not out his knauery laugh at me
when I come home, marry I prithy do q. his M.
and mistris, but whatsoeuer thou seest say nothing
least he be angry and spoile my gown, let me alone
mistris q. he, and so away he goes to York, &
coming to this taylor found him in his shop, &
deliuered him the taffata with this message, that
his mistris had charged him to see it cut out, not y^t
she suspected him, but y^t els he wold let it ly lõg
by him and take other worke in hand, ye taylor
scornfully sayd he should, & asked him if he had
any spectacles about him, no q. the felow my sight
is yoong inough I need no glasses, if you do put
them quoth he, and see if you can see me steale a
yard of taffata out of your mistresse gowne, and so
taking his sheeres in hand, he cut it out so nimbly
that hee cut three foreparts to the gown, and four
side pieces, that by computation / the fellow [E1^v
gest he had stolne two els & a half, but say nothing
he durst. Assoone as he had done, there came in
more gentlemens men with worke, that the taylor
was very busie & regarded not, the seruingmã who
seeing the taylors cloke lying lose, lifted it away &
caried it home with him to his mistris house, where

he discourst to his maister & his mistris what he had seen, & how he had stole the tailors cloake, not to that intent to filch, but to try an experiment vpon him, for maister q. he, when he brings home my mistris gown, he wil complain of ye losse of his cloake, & then see, doe you but tel him that I am experienced in Magike, & can cast a figure, and wil tel him where his cloke is without faile, say but this sir, and let me alone: they al agreed, & resolued to try the wit of their yong man. But leauing him, againe to our taylor: who when he had dispatcht his customers, was ready to walke with one of them to the tauern, & then mist his cloke, searcht al about, but find it he could not, neither knew he whõ to suspect: so with much griefe he past it ouer, & when he had ended the gentlewomans gown (because she was a good customer of his) he himself tooke his nag & rid home withal: welcome he was to the gentlewoman and hir husband, and the gown was passing fit, so that it could not be amended, insomuch that the gentlewoman praisd it, and highly thankt him. Oh mistris (quoth he) though it is a good gown to you, tis an infortunate gowne to me, for that day your man brought the taffata, I had a cloke stoln that stood me but one fortnight before in foure pound, and neuer since could I heare any word of it. Truly said the Gentleman, I am passing sorry for your losse, but that same man that was at your house is passing skilful in Negromancy, and if any man in England can tel you where your cloke is, my man can: marry q. he, and I wil giue him a brace of angels for his labour: so the fellow was cald and talkt with all, and at his mistris request was content to do it, but he would haue his twenty shillings in hand, and promised if he told him not where it was, who had it, and caused it to be deliuered to him again, for his two angels he would giue him ten pounds: vpon this the taylor willingly gaue him the money, and vp went he into a closet like a learned clark, and there was three or foure houres laughing at the taylor, he thinking he had bin al this while at Caurake. At last downe comes the fellow with a figure drawn in a paper in his hand, & smiling cald for a bible, and told the taylor he would tel him who had his cloke, where it was, & helpe him to it againe, so that he would be sworne on a bible to / answer to all questions that he [E2 demanded of him faithfully: the taylor granted and swore on a bible, then hee cõmanded al should go out but his maister, his mistres, the taylor and himself. Then he began thus: wel, you haue taken your oth on the holy bible, tel me q. he, did you not cut three foreparts for my mistris gowne? At this the taylor blusht, & began to be in a chafe, and would haue flung out of the doore, but the seruingman said, nay neuer start man, for before thou goest out of this parlour, if thou deniest it, I wil bring the taffata thou stolest into this place, wrapt in thine own cloake: & therfore answere directly to my question, least to your discredit I shew you the trick of a scholler: the taylor halfe afraid, said he did so indeed: and q he, did you not cut foure side peeces wher you haue cut but two? yes al is true q. the taylor, why then as true it is, that to deceiue the deceiuer is no deceit: for as truly as you stole my mistris taffata, so truly did I steale your cloake, and here it is. At this the taylor was amazed, the gentleman and his wife laught hartily, & so al was turned to a merryment, the taylor had his cloake again, the gentlewoman hir taffata, and the seruing man twenty shillings, was not this prety and witty *Conny-catching* M. *R. G.*

Thus haue I proued to your maships, how there is no estate, trade, occupation, nor mistery, but liues by *Conny-catching*, and that our shift at cards compared to the rest, is the simplest of al, & yet forsooth, you could bestow the paines to write two whole Pamphlets against vs poore conycatchers: think M. *R. G.* it shal not be put vp except you graunt vs our request. It is informed vs that you are in hand with a booke named *The repentance of a Conny-catcher*, with a discouery of secret villainies, wherein you meane to discourse at ful the nature of *the stripping Law*, which is the abuse offered by the Keepers of *Newgate* to poore prisoners, and some that belong to the *Marshalsea*. If you doe so, ye shal do not onely a charitable, but a meritorious deed: for the occasion of most mischiefe, of greatest nipping and foysting, and of al vilanies, comes through the extorting bribery of some coossening and counterfaite keepers and companions, that carry vnlawful warrants about them to take vp men. Wil your worship therfore stand to your worde, and set out the discouery of that, al wee of *Whittington Colledge* wil rest your beadmen. Otherwise looke that I wil haue the crue of *Cony-catchers* sweare themselues your professed enemies for euer. Farewel.

Cuthbert Conny-Catcher.

FINIS.

ERRATA

The following emendations only have been made:—

Page	Line		In the Original reads:—
13	27	'*R. G.*'	'.*RG.*'
18	12	'could'	'cbuld'
21	25–6	'shriking'	'shrikiag'
22	6	'Iustice'	'Instice'
26	7–8	'Miller and his man'	'Miller and his man and his man'
34	15	'*Compostella*'	'*Gompostella*'
34	17	'and'	'and and'
44	13	'to'	'to to'
44	14	'Parish,'	'Parish.'
44	21	'come'	'come come'
46	1	'calues)'	'calues'
46	6	'villainies'	'vill inies'
51	19	'verie'	'vere'
58	11	'*Conny*'	'*Gonny*'
63	4	'giue'	'gine'